The Armchair Paddler

THE ARMCHAIR PADDLER

An Anthology of Canoeing,
Kayaking, and Rafting Adventures

EDITED BY

CECIL KUHNE

Menasha Ridge Press

Printed in the United States of America

Published by Menasha Ridge Press

Distributed by The Globe Pequot Press

First Edition, first printing

Individual Permissions listed on page 230.

Library of Congress Cataloging-in-Publication Data:

Kuhne, Cecil, 1952-

The Armchair Paddler : an anthology of canoeing,

kayaking, and rafting adventures

edited by Cecil Kuhne.

p. cm.

ISBN 0-89732-329-7

1. Canoes and canoeing.

2. Kayaking.

3. Rafting (sports) I. Title

GV783 .K785 2000

797. 12'1--dc21

00-036060

Menasha Ridge Press

2000 First Avenue North, Suite 1400

Birmingham, Alabama 35203

www.menasharidge.com

CONTENTS

Introduction / 1

I. BEGINNINGS

The Lonely Land, by Sigurd F. Olson / 4

The Survival of the Bark Canoe, by John McPhee / 9

Baidarka: The Kayak, by George Dyson / 15

The Starship and the Canoe, by Kenneth Brower / 21

Canoeing With the Cree, by Eric Sevareid / 30

II. BIG DROPS

Rivergods, by Richard Bangs and Christian Kallen / 38

Shiva Winked, by Tim Cahill / 43

Deliverance, by James Dickey / 48

Canyon, by Michael Ghiglieri / 55

Running the Amazon, by Joe Kane / 64

Kayaking the Full Moon, by Steve Chapple / 69

River, by Colin Fletcher / 75

III. THE FAR NORTH

Dangerous River, by R. M. Patterson / 82

Running Wilberforce Canyon, by Bill Mason / 87

Reading the River, by John Hildebrand / 93

Summer North of Sixty, by James Raffan / 104

IV. GRAND CANYON

Broken Waters Sing, by Gaylord Staveley / 110

River Runners of the Grand Canyon, by David Lavender / 118

Romance of the Colorado River, by Frederick S. Dellenbaugh / 124

A River Mystery, by Scott Thybony / 129

V. JOURNEYS ABROAD

Travels With a Kayak, by Whit Deschner / 136

In the Belly of the Earth, by Andrzej Pietowski / 144

A Boat in Our Baggage, by Maria Coffey / 154

Santa Maria!, by Jamie McEwan / 160

VI. OUT TO SEA

Alone at Sea, by Hannes Lindermann / 170

On Celtic Tides, by Chris Duff / 176

Kayaking the Inside Passage, by Byron Ricks / 185

Paddle to the Arctic, by Don Starkell / 193

VII. PRESERVING OUR RIVERS

The Sound of Mountain Water, by Wallace Stegner / 202

Goodbye to a River, by John Graves / 209

The Struggle for a River, by Tim Palmer / 215

There Was a River, by Bruce Berger / 221

About the Contributors / 227

Permissions / 230

INTRODUCTION

AT THIS VERY MOMENT
there are paddlers like you cruising their way along the coast of Maine,
battling the rapids of the Colorado, gliding through the Ozarks, and
drifting down the Nile. There are, no doubt, paddlers etching a splendid
path around Scotland, meandering through Glacier Bay, surfing waves in
New Zealand, and camping on the banks of the Yukon. There are,
undeniably, boaters easing their paddles into the enchanted waters of the
Salmon, the Rio Grande, Lake Superior, and the Mediterranean. And
these are but a few places where this magnificent pastime is practiced.

These paddlers, of course, are fortunate souls. They will enter chasms
whose banks seem to heave straight toward the heavens. They will cruise
across clear alpine lakes and camp on shores illuminated by sunshine
streaming in to warm the white beaches where their tents will be unfurled.

These paddlers will cruise wind-swept ridges and crags of desert
streams. Here the gentle flow of the river will pile itself against precipitous
cliffs and light will dance upon its swirling surface. The air will be as dry
and brittle as the canyon walls which etch the cobalt sky above.

These paddlers will pierce dense forests, steep valleys, imposing bluffs,
mysterious caves, and rushing springs. They will play on ocean tides, and

1

at night peer into pitch-black skies with stars close enough to touch. The rest of the world will seem very far away indeed.

The stories in the collection you have before you are about these special places—and about the unique individuals who ply their waters. The range of experiences described is wide and deep. There are heart-racing tales of derring-do about fierce encounters with whitewater. There are memorable accounts of floats among incredibly pristine streams of Alaska and Canada. And there are inspired journeys through the Grand Canyon, Mexico, Peru, Wyoming, Georgia, Chile, Utah, India, Afghanistan, Ireland, the Atlantic Ocean, and the Inside Passage.

Lastly, there are eloquent pleas to preserve our world's waterways—not only for our sake, but for future generations yet to brush a paddle across this liquid gold. It is, I trust, a compelling collection, and one that I hope inspires you to take a paddle firmly in hand and explore your own infinite—and watery—frontiers.

—Cecil Kuhne

1

BEGINNINGS

THE LONELY LAND

Sigurd F. Olson

The rugged life of the French-Canadian voyageur

THERE ARE FEW PLACES LEFT on the North American continent where men can still see the country as it was before Europeans came and know some of the challenges and freedoms of those who saw it first, but in the Canadian Northwest it can still be done. A thousand miles northwest of Lake Superior are great free rivers, lakes whose horizons disappear, countless unnamed waterways, and ridges and forested valleys still largely unknown. Most of it is part of the Canadian Shield, an enormous outpouring of granitic lava that extends from the bleak coasts of Labrador in the east, almost to the Mackenzie River valley in the west, and then on into the Arctic North.

It is a vast and lonely land, for as yet only its southern fringes have been occupied. The rest is neither settled nor pierced by roads. Though planes have mapped most of it and jets fly high above with vapor trails floating even over the tundras south of the Arctic coast, though a few mining camps serviced by air can be found far in the interior, few men know it well. Hudson's Bay posts and installations of the Royal Canadian Mounted Police are scattered throughout it and at such locations are often found the missions of the Oblate Fathers of Montreal and the Anglican Church of Canada. There are Indian settlements, the Crees and Chippewyans, the

Yellow Knives, the Dog Ribs, and Hares, along the great rivers that have always been their major routes of travel and migration, but the land itself has changed little since the days of the fur trade and exploration.

This was the region the French voyageurs explored and traveled after they knew the country between the St. Lawrence and the Great Lakes. Beyond Lake Superior until 1650, the Northwest was the vast unknown, perhaps the fabled passage to the Pacific, the greatest frontier of the new world. For 200 years these intrepid canoemen probed its farthermost reaches trading wherever they went, establishing posts at strategic points, weaving a vast network of influence over the entire region. During those days fortunes in fur were carried across the portages and paddled down the waterways to satisfy the markets of the east. In the two or three thousand miles between Montreal and the far Northwest, these French Canadians lived and traveled with a spirit, sense of adventure, and pride in their calling that balanced its enormous distances and hardships. These wiry little men—seldom more than five feet four or five—dressed in breech-cloth, moccasins, and leather leggings reaching to thighs, a belted shirt with its inevitable colored pouch for tobacco and a pipe, topped off with a red cap and feather. They were a breed apart. From dawn until dark they paddled their great canoes and packed enormous loads, facing storms, wild uncharted rivers, hostile Indians, and ruthless rivals with a joy and abandon that has possibly never been equaled in man's conquest and exploitation of any new country.

Each spring at the breakup of ice on the St. Lawrence, great brigades of canoes left Montreal for the West, hundreds of gay and colorful craft fashioned from birch-bark, cedar, and spruce. There were the huge 35-foot Montreals with a crew of 14, the Bastard Canoes with a crew of 10, the 25-foot North Canoes and the Half Canoes, for such inland waters as those beyond Grand Portage. Decorated in gaudy designs, each brigade with its own insignia, vermilion-tipped paddles moving in rhythm to the *chansons* of Old France, here was a pageant such as the New World had never known and will never see again.

In command of each brigade was the bourgeois whose word was law. It was he who decided when to start and stop and where to go. In his charge was the precious cargo of trade goods and the responsibility of converting it into fur. These men were usually of Scotch or English origin—Mackenzies, McGillivrays, McTavishes, Simpsons, and McLeods. To them this country and its vast resources were there to be exploited. While they left voluminous diaries and meticulous journals, there is little in them of appreciation of the life they led. To them the country meant fur and fur meant profit. Indians were the means of acquiring it and the voyageurs merely a source of power for the sole purpose of transporting trade goods into the interior and furs back either to Montreal on the St. Lawrence or to York Factory on Hudson Bay. With the exception of a few men such as Peter Pond, Samuel Hearne, or David Thompson, they were seldom impressed with the stark beauty or romance of the land they traversed. To them the fur trade was a business proposition and if at the end of a season the books balanced with a profit, that was all that mattered. Still, without the shrewdness, indomitable will, and vision of these men— the partners and clerks of the various companies, the free traders, and the Bourgeois of the brigades—this commerce would not have developed on the continental scale that it did.

Thousands of men were in the trade from the early 1600s until approximately a hundred years ago. The routes they traveled were as familiar to them as our transcontinental highways are to us. Nothing was thought of leaving Montreal or the Bay for such distant points as Grand Portage on Lake Superior, Cumberland House in the Saskatchewan country, or Fort Chippewyan at the end of Lake Athabasca. A few thousand miles of travel by canoe was as accepted a procedure in those days as taking an automobile trip today.

For a century and a half the French were in control, but after 1760 and the conquest of Canada by the British, the ancient emblem of France, the fleur-de-lis, was seen no more in the far country. Grace Lee Nute says:

Kings came and went, governments rose and fell, wars were fought and boundary lines placed at will, but the border country cared little. Its life went on as before, full of activity, danger, adventure, the struggle of existence, the round of ordinary life in a region that was virtually a law unto itself.

The last century of the trade was a time of fierce competition and the men of the various companies, particularly the North West and Hudson's Bay companies, as well as the free traders, fought bitterly for fur. While it is true the voyageurs sang as they paddled their canoes and made merry with the Indians at the encampments, they also fought pitched battles with their enemies, ambushed rivals and stole their supplies and fur. It was a common practice to intercept bands of Indians taking fur to rival posts, fur that had already been paid for by others. Nothing was thought of piracy or of debauching the Indians with rum to make them amenable. There was bloodshed on lakes and portages, and campsites. Murder went unpunished for there was no law that extended into the hinterlands. The gathering of fur was a deadly serious business to everyone except the voyageurs themselves.

George Simpson of the Hudson's Bay Company must have been very conscious of this as he worked his way up the Churchill in 1820.

Embarked at half past 3 a.m.; passed Fourteen N.W. Canoes. I could not help remarking with much concern the striking contrast between our Brigade and that of our Opponents; all their Canoes are new and well built of good materials, ably manned, a water proof arm chest and cassette for fineries in each, and the baggage covered with new oil cloths, in short well equipped in every respect: on the other hand, our Canoes are old, crazy, and patched up, built originally of bad materials without symmetry and neither adapted for stowage nor expedition; manned chiefly by old infirm creatures or Porkeaters unfit for the arduous duty they have to perform . . . . At four O'Clock observed a half loaded Canoe pushing across the River towards us, it turned out to be Simon McGillivray who merely came alongside to make his observations. This Gentleman I understand has been most active in every nefarious transaction that has taken place in Athabasca, he is notorious for his low cunning, had made Mr. Clarke a prisoner twice and threatens to have him soon again . . . next to Black he is more to be dreaded than any member of the N.W Coy.; he was the principal leader of the lawless assemblage of Halfbreeds and Indian assassins at the Grand Rapid this season; a day of retribution I trust is at hand for this worthy.

With the absorption of the North West Company and other rivals by the Hudson's Bay Company in 1821, competition came to an end. Gradually the trade declined, due partly to the settlement of the west, changing fashions in fur, and because many parts of the country had been exhausted by heavy trapping and hunting. While the Hudson's Bay Company still has far-flung outposts, the old days are gone forever.

All that is left of those colorful days of the past are crumbling forts, old foundations, and the names the voyageurs gave to lakes and rivers and portages. But there is something that will never be lost—the voyageur as a symbol of a way of life, the gay spirit with which he traveled, his singing as he paddled his canoe, and a love of the wilderness that practically depopulated the struggling pioneer settlements along the St. Lawrence during the heyday of the trade.

THE SURVIVAL
OF THE BARK CANOE

John McPhee

The eloquence and surprising sophistication of the native craft

WHEN WHITE EXPLORERS first came to northeastern North America, they looked in wonder at such canoes—as well they might, for nothing like them existed in Europe. There was eloquence in the evidence they gave of the genius of human-kind. The materials were simple, but the structure was not. An adroit technology had come down with the tribes from immemorial time, and now—in the sixteenth, the seventeenth century—here were bark canoes on big rivers and ocean bays curiously circling ships from another world. Longboats were lowered, to be rowed by crews of four and upward. The sailors hauled at their oars. The Indians, two to a canoe, indolently whisked their narrow paddles and easily drew away. In their wake they left a stunning impression. Not only were they faster. They could see where they were going.

White explorers got out of their ships and went thousands of miles in bark canoes. They traveled in them until the twentieth century, for bark canoes were the craft of the north continent. Nothing else, indigenous or imported, could do what they could do. The explorers in the main were not seeking the advancement of geophysical knowledge, chimeric routes to the Orient. They were looking for fur. Fur sources around the Baltic

Sea were diminishing, and prices there had risen to prohibitive levels, so the attention of Western Europe had turned to the American woods. The demand for fur was intense, because it was used not only in pelt form but also, and to a much greater extent, in the making of felt and other materials. Most wanted of all was the fur of the beaver. The underhair, or "beaver wool," had minute barbs, and when the hair was compressed the barbs would hold fabric together.

The fur trade began in the estuaries of rivers. White traders soon followed the Indians upstream to complete their transactions nearer the sources of the fur. What the whites brought to offer were not merely clothes, blankets, beads, and copper kettles but also steel traps, spears, knives, and guns, with which the Indians could vastly increase the collection of fur. Red and white hands were clasped in enterprise. Some Canadians savor the thought that while Americans to the south—intoxicated with their Manifest Destiny—were killing Indians and stealing their land, Canadians red and white were developing warm interracial relationships bonded by a business that was conducted to the advantage of all. All but the beaver. Where Indian families might once have taken just a few pelts for their own use, whole lodges were destroyed. Beaver populations declined toward zero with proximity to the outlets of commerce. Thus the Ojibway, the Cree, the Algonquin—Canadian tribes across the woods—were in on the beginnings of the end of their own environment. They were willing partners, profiteers. Down the river they sold the beaver, the mink, the marten, the lynx, the otter. They sold the hides of deer, moose, caribou. They even sold the skin of the wild goose. They sold anything with hair, almost anything that moved—and to keep the whole bonanza going they sold their birch canoes.

The fur trade, as it lengthened, manifested its own destiny and Canada's, too. The fur trade established canoe routes to the far northwest, and conjoined the segments of a continental wilderness. It is possible to cross Canada by canoe, to crisscross Canada, to go almost anywhere. Canada is 25 percent water. The quantity of it outreaches belief. A sixth of all the fresh water that exists on earth is in Canadian lakes, Canadian ponds, Canadian streams, Canadian rivers. A friend of mine who grew up in Timmins, a remote community in Ontario, once told me about an Indian friend of his in boyhood who developed an irresistible urge to see New York City. He put his canoe in the water and started out. From stream to lake to pond to portage, he made his way a hundred miles to Lake Timiskaming, and its outlet, the Ottawa River. He went down the Ottawa to the St. Lawrence, down the St. Lawrence to the Richelieu, up the Richelieu to Lake Champlain, and from Lake Champlain to the Hudson. At the Seventy-ninth Street Boat Basin, he left the canoe in the custody of attendants and walked on into town. Reversing that trip, and then some, one could go by canoe from Seventy-ninth Street to Alaska, and down the Yukon to the Bering Sea. By the Rat-Porcupine route (up the Rat, down the Porcupine), the length of the portage over the Rocky Mountains is half a mile. Between the Atlantic and the Pacific, anywhere on the routes that were used by the fur trade, the longest portage is thirteen miles (and even that is an exaggeration, because the trail is interrupted by a mile-long lake). In 1778, a white trader for the first time crossed that portage. It is Methye Portage, in what is now northern Saskatchewan. His name was Peter Pond. Beyond the portage, in the region of Lake Athabasca, he encountered a crowded population of beaver whose fur (as a result of the mean temperature there) was as long and rich as any yet found in North America. The discovery extended to its practical limit the distance that fur could travel in the unfrozen season by canoe from the source to Montreal. Transatlantic ships could navigate the St. Lawrence to the Lachine Rapids, near Montreal. At the head of the rapids, the fur-trade canoe routes began. The distance from Lachine to Lake Athabasca was three thousand miles. Unsurprisingly, the men who did the paddling were known as the voyageurs.

Some stayed in the far-northern outposts for the winter, others in Montreal. With the spring breakup, they started from both ends, and by midsummer had met in the middle. They exchanged cargoes. These were some of the things in the packs bound west and north: false hair, garters, tomahawks, rolls of bark from the birches of the East. The voyageurs returned—the survivors returned—whence they had come. Crosses marked their routes, sometimes many crosses in a single place. Packs weighed 90 pounds, and a voyageur on a portage was responsible for 6. Generally, two packs were portaged at a time, and sometimes three. The largest recorded burden carried by one man in one trip across a portage was 630 pounds. It has been reported that the voyageurs liked to show off. They were, on the whole, small men; large ones were not worth their extra weight in fur. Even under the hundred-and-eighty-pound weight of a standard two-pack load, they were more or less forced to run if they wanted to move at all, so they took off at a trot at the start of a portage—uphill, downhill, over rough or boggy terrain. They died of strangulated hernias, and of heart attacks, sometimes. Five hundred mink skins would fit in one pack. Voyageurs also drowned in rapids.

When they started out in the spring from Montreal, they were blessed by a priest, and each canoe was given a summer-ration eight-gallon keg of brandy. The voyageurs drank most of it the first night out. They went virtually nowhere the next day. Sober again, they sang their way to Lake Superior. All day, they sang chansons of the Loire Valley, which gave them their rhythm and their distraction. They went up the Ottawa and up the Mattawa and across the Height of Land. They went down the French River from Lake Nipissing to Georgian Bay. They circled the north rim of Lake Superior. They averaged fifty miles a day. When rivers became too shallow for paddling, they shoved upcurrent with poles. When they could not pole, they got out and lined—hauled the canoes, bargelike, from the shore with ropes. When they could not line, they dragged. They would do anything to avoid a portage or reduce its length. There were more than a hundred portages between Lake Athabasca and Montreal.

They wore plumed bats, billowing shirts, bright-colored sashes. Their paddle blades were brilliant red, green, blue. They stopped once an hour for a churchwarden smoke, and they measured big lakes not in miles but in pipes. They got up in the morning at two or three. Hours of paddling preceded breakfast. They made their camp at nine, even ten, at night. In the north, they ate pemmican-pounded buffalo or caribou meat, sometimes with berries in it, dried in the sun. In the Middle West, they ate wild rice and maize. Toward the East, they ate pork and hardtack, peas and beans.

They came in large numbers from the Quebecois farm country east of Montreal, like the forebears of Henri Vaillancourt. From the fur trade the voyageurs got almost nothing but a change of scene, in a business that for its owners was unimaginably profitable. An investment of, say, 800 pounds could bring back 16,000. The voyageurs worked for the North West Company and, ultimately, for the Hudson's Bay Company, which merged the North West Company out of existence in 1821.

Bark canoes the Indians made for themselves seldom exceeded 20 feet, and were generally shorter than that, on down to 9-foot and 10-foot hunter canoes. Canoes they built on order for the fur trade were 36 feet long and could carry 4 tons. It took four men to portage them. Wet, they weighed 600 pounds. They were known as *canots de maitre*. They traveled in brigades—usually four, but sometimes as many as ten, in a line. The bowman, the *avant*, had the captain role. In white water, the sternman, the *gouvernail*, was too far back to see what the voyageurs called the *fil d'eau*— the place to shoot the rapid. Paddlers in the middle worked two abreast. Personnel shifts (advancement, transfer, death) caused a crew to vary considerably, and as many as 15 men sometimes paddled a *canot de maitre*. Eight or ten was the usual number. The crew slept under the overturned canoe and an attached tarpaulin, and to make this arrangement as spacious as possible the canoes were designed with high, curling ends. For the more northerly runs through what is now Manitoba and Saskatchewan, the trade developed the *canot du nord*, which was narrower and shorter—25 feet. Some of the streams of the northern route were too small for the *canot de maitre*. The companies appropriated the art from the Indians, set up their own factories, and made bark canoes. On spruce-plank building beds with permanent stake holes, the plant at Trois-Rivieres, Quebec, could produce in a year 20 *canots de maitre*. Certain white names ultimately acquired celebrity in the field, notably L. A. Christopherson, who for almost 40 years built, and in part designed, Hudson's Bay Company fur-trade canoes. High on their curling sterns were the letters "HBC." This, in company argot, meant "Here Before Christ."

BAIDARKA: THE KAYAK

George Dyson

The development of the first kayaks made from skin and wood

TWO DISTINCT GROUPS OF people made the shores of the eastern North Pacific their home: those who built dugout canoes and those who built skin boats. All the contrasts between virgin rain forest and barren island were reflected in their opposing techniques, yet the resulting vessels displayed equally sparse and graceful lines. The dugout builders took an enormous chunk of wood and eliminated everything, down to splinters, that was not essential to their definition of a boat. The skin-boat people, working in reverse, began their boats from splinters, piecing together a framework that delineated the bare minimum of their vessel. The dugout, of living cedar, was a creature of the forest. The baidarka, of driftwood, whalebone, and sea-lion skin, was entirely a creature of the sea.

The skin boat was a circumpolar concept. Along all northern coastlines, and on inland waterways as well, these craft ranged southward as far as materials, climate, and hostile forest-dwellers would permit. A hundred and fifty years ago Russian adventurers carried baidarkas with them on winter expeditions to Mexico, Hawaii, and even Micronesia, only to find the otherwise serviceable skin boats rendered useless as the equatorial sun melted the whale-fat waterproofing from their seams. Even in the refrigerated north, the skin boat's biodegradable components left archaeologists with scarcely a trace. We cannot be sure who were the first builders of these craft or when it was that the Aleuts—or pre-Aleuts—began paddling to and from their remote outposts in the sea.

The earliest known settlements among the Aleutian Islands date back more than eight thousand years. The skin boat might have migrated to the Aleutians from somewhere else, or it might have been invented there independently, perhaps in a period of post-glacial isolation, as the rising sea level forced land-based nomadic hunters to put their ice age-sharpened minds and tools to building boats. The kayak's ancestry can be traced to a practice evidenced among landlocked hunting cultures of both Asia and America: stuffing an animal skin with willow branches as an improvised, spur-of-the-moment boat.

"They say that their forefathers came from their original dwelling-places in the west [Asia]," wrote the missionary and pioneer Alaskan ethnologist Ivan Veniaminov, concerning the origins of the Aleuts.

> In that country there were no storms, no winters, but constant pleasant atmosphere, and the people lived peaceably and quietly; but in the course of time quarrels and intertribal wars compelled them to move farther and farther to the eastward, until they finally reached the seacoast. Later they were even compelled to take to the water. But even on the coast they could not remain in peace, being pressed by other people, and therefore were compelled to seek refuge on the islands; and finally, traveling from island to island, they settled in their present villages.

At the time of Vitus Bering's arrival in 1741, the Aleuts are estimated to have numbered between 10,000 and 20,000, more than the aboriginal population of the Ohio Valley, Florida, New York State, or New England. The Aleutian Islands were barren but the sea around them was rich. Until less than 250 years ago, the population existed in "pre-contact" times. Two hundred years ago, after contact had been made, the northwest coast of America still was shifting unpredictably from map to map. When

Captain Cook arrived on the Alaskan Coast in 1778, he found that the latest maps he had brought with him from Europe showed some of the Aleutian Islands intentionally misplaced—by secretive Russian fur merchants who wished to keep the islands to themselves.

Yermak's campaign across Siberia in the 1580s had led the way for Russian fur hunters to reach the Pacific Coast. Spreading across hundreds of thousands of square miles, with fewer than a thousand men, Yermak's band of Cossacks succeeded in one of the greatest conquests of enemy territory the world has ever seen. Supplied with weapons, food, and encouragement by the merchants of the Stroganov family, Yermak's Cossacks were, according to an agreement paraphrased by Richard Pierce, "to pay for the supplies from their spoils, or, if they perished during the expedition, they were to redeem the expenses incurred by the Stroganovs by prayer in the next world." Within fifty years or so, Yermak's followers and their descendants—with an added measure of criminals, political exiles, and adventurous camp-followers thrown in—reached the Pacific Coast, and, under similar contracts with their merchant backers, some of them began building crudely sewn-together vessels and taking to the sea.

Sea-otter pelts, each worth a small fortune in trade with the Chinese, were what led these Russian *promyshlenniks*, or fur hunters, to willingly accept the risks. If the treacherous Pacific cast them upon some unknown—and thus otter-infested—reef, some of the crew paid with their lives while others divided an increased share of pelts.

As the Russians pushed eastward toward America along the Aleutian chain, at every inhabited island they were greeted by vessels made from skins. The word *baidara*, a term originating on the rivers of the Ukraine, was used to describe the natives' larger, open, skin-covered craft, while the diminutive of this, *baidarka*, referred to the distinctively hatched, smaller species of decked skin boat. The Russians commandeered all available baidarkas to hunt sea otters on their behalf, and demanded that more of them be built. The larger baidaras, too clumsy for the hunt, were confiscated to carry supplies, and to prevent the men from launching a mass attack or taking their families with them and making an escape. Armed resistance was hopeless, and any insurrection brought swift and bloodthirsty revenge. The aboriginal culture suffered wholesale upheaval and entire settlements collapsed. "God is high above, and the Czar is far away," was the unofficial motto of the campaign. Only cooperative Aleuts who served the Russian purpose were able to survive, saved by the skin of their boats.

The Russians were landsmen. Whether merchants or exiles, most arrived at Okhotsk on foot. The vessels that transferred them to Kamchatka, then along the Aleutian Islands and finally to mainland Russian America, were crude galiot-rigged craft, centuries behind their time. The Russian skippers practiced only the rudiments of navigation, blindly "following the fence" from island to island, often returning without knowing exactly where they had been. Shipwreck was all too common and near-escape the rule.

So it was that the Russians cast their lot with the Aleuts. They lived in Aleut semi-subterranean dwellings, ate Aleut food, took Aleut wives with whom they had half-Aleut children, and depended on Aleut boats. In their dependence on the baidarka, the Russians appropriated the central element in the culture of the Aleuts. In the shape of the baidarka, Aleut ethnology and technology were inseparably intertwined. The Russians could not get the one without the other; they began to see things from an Aleut frame of mind.

The Russians widened the baidarka's beam along with its use, and extended its length as well as its range. Before the traffic in skins wiped out their local sea otters, the Aleuts had had no need to forage any great distance from their homes. They had carried little with them beyond the implements of the hunt, attached securely to the baidarka's narrow deck. Their boats were not designed for the bulky spoils of Russian trade. Until Russians grew tired of paddling—making the rounds of subjugated islands collecting furs for themselves and the czar—there had been little reason to add a passenger's manhole in the center of the Aleut boats.

Before their conversion to the Russian Orthodox faith, the Aleuts needed no three-hatch baidarkas to carry around the fathers of the church. Their own shamans and wizards either flew from island to island in supernatural form, or paddled their own boats.

The baidarka and its Aleut paddlers provided the Russians with a means of communication along stretches of coastline inaccessible to any other craft. The logistics defy comparison; the advance of the Russian baidarka fleets constituted as detailed a survey by a foreign power as the North Pacific has ever known. By comparison, the British and American traders merely touched the surface of the northwest coast. "This boat and the Aleuts who supplied its motive power were the key to Russian activity during the entire pre-1867 period," writes Richard Pierce, who has translated and edited many of the Russian sources here. "Without these auxiliaries, the Russians would have had to content themselves with trading, as did the New Englanders on the coast . . . With this very adaptable form of locomotion the Russians were able to live much closer to the land and its inhabitants. Almost anywhere they went, for hunting or exploration, they depended on the baidarka."

At the turn of the nineteenth century, fleets of six and seven hundred baidarkas were sweeping annually across the Gulf of Alaska, the ranks of Koniag, Chugach, and Aleut paddlers tightened into close formation by a mutual fear of the mainland's Tlingit tribes. The journey was hard on the boats and tougher on the men. After a storm or enemy attack, crippled baidarkas were cannibalized to repair the less seriously injured craft. The survivors spent the winter building new boats in preparation for the next year's hunt. Baidarkas were being built by the thousands in the Russian-American colonies for close to one hundred years.

The design of the baidarka was never fixed. It varied according to fashion, adapted to changing function, and, above all, it searched for speed. Minute attention was paid to subtle differences in each baidarka's streamlined curves. The Gulf of Alaska, with its endless succession of storms and shallow, tide-swept seas, tank-tested the results of the baidarka's "genetic drift." Even during the final years of the sea-otter hunt, with American support vessels and repeating firearms appearing on the scene, the baidarka still earned its living through outmaneuvering one of the most evasive creatures of the sea.

The Russian hunters and explorers brought the baidarka to mainland North America more than two centuries ago, one step at a time along the Aleutian chain. When Russian America was ceded to the United States in 1867, the baidarka was thrown in as part of the deal, with fifty years or so left before the baidarka and the sea otter together grew commercially extinct. The next step in this chain of events is up to us, as heirs to a technology the Russians first learned from the Aleuts. I foresee a renaissance of the baidarka, reconstructed out of inanimate materials for purposes beside the hunt. But first we must look back, at the record left by the baidarka in the course of finding its way into our hands.

THE STARSHIP AND THE CANOE

Kenneth Brower

The modern-day re-creation of the ancient Aleutian kayak

NORTHWEST OF GLACIER Bay in Alaska, where the Inside Passage ends, Eskimo country begins, and the dugout gives way to the skin boat. The Eskimos, and their cousins the Aleuts, were a rude people, compared to the sculptors and carpenters of the Inside Passage, but they were better seamen. They had no interconnected system of inland fiords, no bulwark of seaward archipelagos, to protect them from the North Pacific. They ventured into that moody, storm-breeding sea in canoes so light they could be carried under one arm. Made of animal skin stretched over wood frames, Eskimo boats were simple, easy to repair, shock-resistant, beautiful, and fast. Eskimo umiaks, large open vessels, carried tremendous loads and as many as 40 people. Eskimo kayaks, slender and nearly weightless, were the finest hunting canoes in history. Skin boats made the Eskimo culture circumpolar, extending its reach over the northernmost coasts of Asia, America, and Greenland. The oars of the umiaks and the double-bladed paddles of the kayaks chopped down vast distances, allowing Eskimos to exchange ideas, designs, and genes all around the top of the world. A Greenland Eskimo could follow, haltingly, the speech of an Eskimo from western Alaska. It was not that way in the dugout country. When a Tsimshian addressed a Nootka, he might as well have been speaking Chinese, or Kwakiutl.

21

Other peoples have experimented with skin boats. In Europe the Celts built them. The Irish went to sea in a sort of umiak as recently as Elizabethan times, and they still paddle the cowhide curragh on lakes. Next to the kayak, this curragh, oval, dumpy, and slow, is a sorry performance.

Kayak design varied. In the Gulf of Alaska, where big storm waves came up suddenly, the kayaks were built strong and seaworthy. In northern Alaska, where offshore pack ice narrowed the reach, and where the hunters had to navigate thin leads in the ice, kayaks were built light, slim, and low-sided. Materials varied. The Greenland Eskimos covered their kayaks with seal skin, the Canadian Eskimos with caribou skin, the Aleuts with sea-lion skin. The Eskimos used bearded seal when they could get it, and walrus when they couldn't. For frames, most Eskimos used wood, but not the caribou Eskimos of the central Arctic. No trees grew on their tundra. What scraps they had were driftwood and they were ignorant of its origin. They believed that trees grew like kelp in undersea forests, which storms uprooted and washed ashore. They made their kayak skeletons by reassembling in a somewhat changed order the skeletons of whales.

For the frame of his first canoe, George picked aluminum. For the skin he picked fiberglass.

"In my travels and experience with heavy craft requiring the use of sails or machinery," he has written, "I soon realized that much of the British Columbia coastline was either inaccessible or posed extreme danger to such vessels. Most of British Columbia's vast system of open coast and intricate tidal waterways is outside the limits of what is considered a safe path for modern travel and can be viewed only briefly and at a distance through such means."

After *D'Sonoqua* George had worked on a number of big boats requiring the use of sail or machinery. He remembered some fondly but had no desire to build or own one. He was bothered not just by their breadth of beam and the depth they drew, but by their financial encumbrances.

Several of George's friends owned boats and tried to scratch out livings with them, and all these friends were in trouble with the bank.

In Vancouver with George I visited one such friend, a man named Dave. Dave was a former dope smuggler who had gone straight. He was now master of the *Barbara B.*, a tiny cargo vessel. We found *Barbara B.* moored in the shadow of one of the city's bridges. The light was dim, the air was cavelike, and the traffic shook the bridge high above us. (George Dyson's Vancouver is like that—shadowy and out of the way. He seems to transact most of his business under freeways or on decaying wharves.) Dave, the captain, was a bald man with a full black beard, which the uncertainties of the dope game and the boat business had rimed with gray. He had been on the receiving end of his old smuggling operation when he fell in love with the vessels bringing in his contraband. *Barbara B.* was his first command. He had got her with only $500 and some fast talk at the bank. He greeted George full of good news. He had a new partner up in Union Bay, he said. The partner was a wheeler-dealer, a hustler, an expert at juggling A and B fishing licenses, that sort of thing, but the man had a heart of gold. The new partner wanted to serve the communities up there, and *Barbara B.* was going to be the ship. They were going to process fresh fish—salmon, cod, halibut, crabs, prawns, everything—and send it down to Vancouver on *Barbara B.* Dave was going to steam north soon to scout out the place. There was, believe it or not, George (said Dave), a machine shop up there. Or so Dave had heard. The potatoes in Union Bay, Dave understood, cost less than in Vancouver. That was a very good sign, Dave thought.

Dave's mate was a stocky, red-bearded man in overalls and no shirt. He kept his meaty arms folded in front of him. He looked surly and said nothing. He did not look bright. I wondered if he was Dave's enforcer from the old days. He seemed to watch us with suspicion.

We drank herb tea in the low-ceilinged, handmade galley, over a table surfaced with a chart of the British Columbia coast. Then we said goodbye. George and I walked down the plank and away from the boat.

I had noticed that George did not seem to share Dave's enthusiasm. "Sounds pretty encouraging," I ventured. George made an unintelligible sound. I asked if *Barbara B.* wasn't a good boat. Yes, she was a good boat, he answered—she had a big hold—but she was in trouble with the bank. It was in watching people like Dave, George said, that he had decided he wanted no part of the big-boat business.

"It was the use of the light seagoing canoe," he writes, "which once enabled people to live and travel throughout this coastline, instead of in the present pattern of centralization at the few areas offering facilities for modern transport and communication. I could see that this presently extinct manner of travel was the one which offered me a chance for the closer contact I sought to establish with this coast, and I began to accumulate all available information on canoe travel throughout the world's history.

"The canoe must be fast in order to deal with strong tidal currents and to make the greatest use of this coast's limited periods of predictable and favorable conditions for crossing long stretches of open water. It must be as light as possible in order to be easily propelled in the water and carried safely ashore in the many areas where no anchorage or shelter for heavy craft exists. If it is inherently stable without ballast or keel it may survive heavy weather at sea by being tossed harmlessly out of the way of large breaking waves, avoiding the heavy-keeled craft's habit of remaining tragically fixed at the advance of a destructive mass of water. If an open canoe is given the freeboard necessary to remain safe in unskilled hands and rough waters it will possess so much windage as to require much extra effort against the least breeze, so it is advantageous to lower the freeboard and achieve safety by decking the canoe and seating the paddlers in individual manholes. The low profile and center of gravity of such a decked canoe can be stabilized with very little beam, and an exceptionally narrow, efficient, and easily driven craft results. The fine lines of such a craft pass easily through and among rough waters, and safe travel in these conditions is possible, along with the ability to land on open beaches through heavy surf. The little sail needed to drive such a craft when winds permit can be carried without need for ballast or fixed rigging, and easily hoisted or stowed as desired.

"It was necessary for me to consider all possible materials and methods, and make the compromises which occur between ideal design and practical technique. The form I had in mind had much in common with those developed by the Aleuts and Eskimos, and I studied their adaptable and efficient pattern of construction involving a light flexible frame covered with a tough waterproof skin. It was this combination of independently flexible frame and skin which enabled their otherwise light and frail craft to withstand the stresses of the stormy, shallow, and ice-filled northern seas.

"Their boats were pieced together from bone, driftwood, and animal hides and were greatly limited by this in their size, strength, and durability. By adapting their highly evolved methods to presently available and superior materials I arrived at a workable system. Aluminum tubing is lashed strongly but flexibly together to form a frame, which is covered with a waterproof and durable skin of laminated glass-reinforced poly resin. This produces a stronger, lighter, and more easily fabricated hull than any existing process known to boatbuilding, although it is similar to some present methods of building aircraft."

George's first fiberglass kayak was sixteen feet long, modeled on a kayak from Nunivak Island. He first tried to cover the frame with a green fabric, but he couldn't get the material taut. The Eskimos had sewn their skins on raw and wet and let them shrink tight, but the green fabric would not behave that way. When it failed, George settled on fiberglass. He copied the kayak's lines directly from *The Bark Canoes and Skin Boats of North America*, by Chapelle and Adney. This book is George's bible. The authors had begun it from concern with the speed at which skin boats decay in museums. "The purpose of the study," wrote Chapelle, "was to measure the skin boats and to make scale drawings that would permit the construction of a replica exact in details of appearance, form, construction, and also in working behavior." George did so, following the Nunivak Eskimos in everything but materials.

The Nunivak kayak had a single large manhole in which a passenger sat with his back to the paddler's. George's version proved tippy, and today he is embarrassed by it. He continues to use it for short errands, though, and its skin shows not a single dent from a career of rough use on stony beaches.

George looked around for a better model.

The best of the old kayaks, according to Chapelle, were those of the Alaskans and the Greenlanders. Kayaks from Asia and the Canadian Arctic were not nearly so good. Of the two superior genera of kayaks, Greenland's needle-tipped boats were decked with more elaborate equipment than Alaska's, but the quality of the basic design was about the same. Alaska was closer to George, so his attention turned there. The best of the Alaskan kayaks were made by the Aleuts, he learned. The Aleuts handled their kayaks better than anyone in the world.

The Aleuts were master kayakers out of necessity. The Aleutian Islands have one of the dreariest climates on earth. When gales are not whipping the islands, dense fogs are smothering them softly. The Aleutians seldom see direct sunlight. In all the chain, there are only two stands of trees, small groves of Sitka spruce planted by white men a century and a half ago, still stunted today. Before these sad little plantations, the wind howled over the islands without a single obstruction. Aleutian birds hug the ground. Aleutian insects have lain so low for so long that the wings of some species have atrophied. Aleutian people lived in communal lodges buried for warmth in the tundra.

The caribou Eskimos of the Canadian Arctic were treeless and wind-swept too, but they had caribou. The Aleuts, aside from a few edible plants, nesting birds, and bird eggs, had only a cruel sea. They went out into it with an arsenal: sinew-backed bows, bone-tipped arrows, dart throwers, spear throwers, bolos, harpoons, bird spears, and lances. They brought back seals, sea lions, sea otter, sea cows, whales, ducks, geese, loons, murres, cormorants. They fished for halibut and cod with 150-fathom lines braided from the stalks of giant kelp. They caught flounder with small hooks of shell.

The artistic dugout-builders of the Inside Passage hated to leave sight of land, and they ventured over the horizon only when a harpooned whale towed them there, or when a storm blew them. The Aleut kayakers paddled over the horizon regularly, and on purpose. They made casual trips to the Kamchatka Peninsula in Asia. It may be, in fact, that the Aleut racial divergence from the Eskimo is because of intermarriage with Kamchatka natives. The Aleuts may not have been highbrow, but they were cosmopolitan.

The Aleuts' sea-otter hunts were cooperative. From four to 20 kayaks, some with one manhole, some with two, fanned out in a semicircle. When a hunter saw an otter surfacing for air, he pointed with his paddle, and the kayaks converged on the spot. When the otter surfaced again, it was greeted by a barrage of stone darts. These were cast with the added leverage of a throwing board, and each was connected by a line to a seal-bladder float, which impeded the wounded otter's escape and marked its position. The kayaks kept pace easily with the fleeing float. The pursuit added interest to the otter's oxygen debt, and it had to come to the surface to pay off. When it did, the kayaks were gathered in a tight circle around the float, and the throwing boards were cocked once again.

The otter were hunted also in two-man kayaks with bow and arrow. One man was the archer, the other carried a long pole fitted at the end with crosspieces, like a brush, with which he fished out the arrows. The archer might miss, but would succeed in driving the otter underwater before it could draw a full breath. The hunters followed the tiring otter by watching the bubbles.

The Aleuts killed their whales with poisoned lances. First they prepared their souls, through the arduous ritual that always preceded Native American whaling, then they smeared their lances with a deadly extract from the roots of monkshood, a dark-cowled flower common in the

Aleutians. At least two canoes went out. If one was smashed by flukes, the other could come to the rescue. The hunters approached the whale cautiously from the rear. They threw their lances, blew on their hands in superstition, and paddled like hell in the other direction. The poison killed the whale in a few days, and if the hunters were lucky the body drifted ashore.

In Aleut kayaks, the rims of the manholes were fitted with waterproof skirts of intestine, which the paddler drew tight around his chest and tied in a bow. In addition, he wore an intestine parka with drawstrings at the neck and sleeves. When he had knotted his last drawstring, the hunter was truly embarked. Man and kayak became a watertight unit, a sea centaur. If a wave flipped the kayak, the paddler knew how to right it. He had techniques for retrieving a paddle lost while he was upside down under water, then righting the canoe with it. He even had a technique for righting the canoe with no paddle at all. Today, Greenland Eskimos practice ten different rolls designed to meet ten different contingencies at sea, and it is likely that the Aleuts were as well drilled and as acrobatic. They, like the Greenlanders, were expert at rolling deliberately to duck the force of a breaking wave. They played in the surf like sea lions.

The Aleuts could repair serious damage to a kayak without coming ashore. Just as porpoises come to the aid of wounded or sick pod members, supporting them at the surface with blowholes above the water, so two healthy kayaks would float side by side while the sick one was lifted from the sea and laid lengthwise across their decks, where the damage could be mended.

The Aleut's boots had soles of sea-lion flipper and uppers of sea-lion esophagus. Under his intestine rain parka was a second parka of sea-lion hide. He could no longer call his epidermis his own. He imitated the structure of sea mammals in building his boats. Paddling, his heart beat within a framework of artificial ribs inspired by those creatures. He fed on fish. He was as easy in the water as the animals he borrowed designs and materials from. His ease was not instinctive; it had to be taught him by his elders, but so it is for most of the other warm-blooded animals that have returned to the ocean. It is hard to devise a definition for sea mammal that does not make the Aleut a specimen. When the naturalist George Steller, who accompanied Vitus Bering to Alaska in 1741, saw his first Aleut, a man kayak-shaped below the waist, sea-lioned and bird-feathered above, with sun-darkened face and bone in nose, the naturalist was seeing a new species.

Russian fur-hunters followed Bering to the Aleutians, searching for fur seal and sea otter. They named the Aleut umiak the baidar. The kayak they called by the diminutive, baidarka.

CANOEING WITH THE CREE

Eric Sevareid

A 2,250-mile journey from Minneapolis to Hudson Bay, made in 1930
by the famous broadcaster when he was 17

AS WE ENTERED THE HARBOR,
filled with islands and rocks, we drew up alongside a big boat in which an
Indian was fishing. He was short and stocky, dressed in black trousers and
moccasins, covered with rubbers, as was the summer custom. He looked
astonishingly like a white man and spoke almost perfect English. His
name was Willie Everett and, we later learned, he was pure Cree. He knew
English because his father as well as himself had been a "Hudson Bay
Indian" or a "tripper," an Indian who works solely for the company, on
the trail most of the time.

Willie was our constant companion during our day at Berens River. At
supper that night, on a small island to which he directed us, he sat cross-
legged beside us, drank our tea, and ate our chocolate. Between puffs on
his big pipe, he told us stories of the "bush country," stories that kept us
awake many hours, despite the fact that were very tired.

As we lay in our blankets, knowing that several hundred people were
around us, but knowing not a thing about the place we were in, we
watched the flashing, colored northern lights which sometimes extended
far to the south. And somewhere, on the dark mainland, people were
playing a phonograph. The music floated across the bay to us and made
us feel comfortable inside.

The light of the gray dawn revealed across the water a low, square, white building, trimmed with red—the Hudson Bay post of Berens River. It was the first of the several posts that grew to be havens of rest and information for us. The "company" store in each district is the center of all official life and the gathering place of natives and whites alike from the several hundred square miles of trapping, hunting, and prospecting wilderness that it serves. The Hudson Bay men, together with the Mounted Police, hold absolute rule over the northland.

Herb Cowan had given us a letter to the post manager. He was away. We met, however, the two young "clarks," as the assistants are known, although much of their labor is making trips by dog team or canoe, freighting flour and other necessities.

In the company of Willie Everett, who was all dressed up for Sunday, we followed the twisting, well-beaten paths through the settlement and strolled among the tiny, mud-calked cabins in which the Crees lived. We strolled at a slow pace, while Willie described to us the varieties of spruce and pine around us and expounded at length upon the soothing effects of balsam pitch when applied to a cut or bruise—something we remembered.

We were walking directly behind a group of six or seven young Indian girls with their mother. They spoke among themselves in Cree, at the same time laughing and giggling merrily. Walt and I couldn't help but feel uncomfortable, since we were certain they were directing their humor at us with our peculiar boots and hats and breeches, but Willie said they were just remarking upon the excellent odor from his pipe. They were wishing they could have a smoke. They all smoke, even the old women and the little children.

After they had switched off on another path we could hear them whistling loudly, although we could not see them. According to our guide they were whistling for us, but our inclination to follow them was absolutely at zero.

It takes many years for a people accustomed to centuries of the wild forest life to completely adopt the customs of civilization. Because Berens

River is close to the cities of the south and because the steamers stop regularly, these girls wore the same type of clothes that the city girls wear. But their natural grace had disappeared, hampered by an unnatural apparel. They walked awkwardly in their patent-leather shoes, even though they were flat-footed. They wore their clothing with a stiff erectness; their skirts and blouses were ill-fitting and, indeed, all the beauty that should have been theirs was spoiled.

We had intended to go to church in the Methodist mission building, but the doors were closed when we arrived. On the way Willie stopped several old, lined squaws and chatted with them. Some of them shook hands with us.

"Those are the real old squaws," Willie said. "Look how their toes turn in when they walk. The Indians don't walk like that any more."

Everyone was wearing dress moccasins, low-cut slippers with heavy beading adorning them. During the week, and always when on the trail, they wear the ankle-length footgear which is not so ornate. Most of the men wore some combination of different suits of clothes, for the Sabbath. On the trail they stick to their overall, blue denim cloth which is excellent for summer bush travel, for it is warm, takes a long time to soak through, and lasts forever.

One does not have to visit California to see a nudists' colony. There is one in every Indian settlement in Canada, at least as far as the boys from the age of six to 20 are concerned. Of course, they don't go about the camp unclothed, but when they get to the "ol' swimming hole," there's only one way to swim and that's in the "raw." We watched them a while and finally Willie coaxed one into diving for us, for a snapshot. Holding his nose he sprawled through the air like a frog and hit the water, mostly on his stomach. It was strange that boys like that, living near the water all their lives, should be such poor swimmers.

Then we met the chief—Chief Berens himself, ruler over some three hundred Crees. The chief had been elected at the annual treaty, Willie informed us. He was to hold the title for three years. So far, he had been on the throne for 15 years and had no thought of retiring. The trouble was, Willie said sadly, that the chief was such a fiery old reprobate, such a crafty politician, and such a fast talker when anyone had courage enough to oppose him, that he turned his office into a real dictatorship. To be frank, he said, all the other braves were scared of him.

But the Hudson Bay clerks told us that night that perhaps Willie was just a little envious of the chief's reputation and position. Although Willie did look the more handsome and intelligent and although Willie could speak the better English, the chief was just the sort of man who was needed to handle the sometimes unruly Berens tribe.

Not in his wigwam, surrounded by his squaw and papooses, involved in consultation with his medicine men, did we find the chief. No. He was reclining in a most undignified position in a frayed and dirty hammock, under a tree in his front yard, smoking, not a peace pipe, but a foul, black instrument that moved about between his lips as though it had been there for years and years—and it had. He was very interesting. He shook hands solemnly, asked after our health in a nice manner and chatted with us for a quarter of an hour on many subjects. Yes, he had heard of Minneapolis.

We liked Chief Berens. He bore his position with just the right amount of dignity. He had a fine sense of his place, but I cannot say that of some of the white men and women who stepped off the steamer to stare at the Indians. They gathered about the chief in a circle and asked him silly questions like, "Do you have any papooses?" Some of them actually held out pieces of candy, as though he were a bear in a zoo!

We wandered over to the forestry station and met all the young chaps there, the airplane pilot, the radio operators, the pigeon trainer, and the cook. They were a splendid bunch. All of them young and strong and intelligent. The more we traveled the more we discovered that it is the young white men that rule the north. Up in an elevated box roost strutted a score or more of beautiful carrier pigeons. One man spends his entire time training them. Every time a plane went out on fire patrol, on a mapping flight, or for any purpose, a pair of birds went along in a cage. Two are carried, because sometimes a hawk will get one of them.

Just a few days before we reached Berens River the seaplane there had been forced to land on a little isolated lake far in the wilderness. Both pigeons got back with the news of a broken propeller, Winnipeg was radioed, a plane was out with a new propeller, and the men were back in the settlement at dusk.

We had been pretty proud of the *Sans Souci*, until these men caught sight of it. She was a big, strong, well-balanced craft, if you were to ask us. But how they laughed when they lifted it.

"How could you come so far in a little cockleshell like that?" one of them asked.

As they were inspecting our boat and slim little paddles, another fellow strode up and said, "Say, let me try her once." He wore no shirt and never have I seen such well developed arms, or such a big chest on a moderate-sized man.

He tried the *Sans Souci*, with one of our paddles. It was as though he had a motor on the end. Across the bay and through the reeds the canoe shot like a racing boat. Walt and I just looked at each other. We had developed a pretty good opinion of our own ability by that time, but we were babes compared with this man. As he rammed her prow high up in the mud with one thrust of the blade, one of the "clarks" leaned over and whispered to us, "He's a Mountie."

Well, that explained it!

Private Alfred Jones was the first mountie we had ever met. I had read about them, dreamed about them since I was a little kid, and had ached to meet one in the flesh. That was the biggest thrill I had received from meeting anyone since the time I shook hands with Jack Dempsey himself, and swore I wouldn't wash my right hand for a week. We also met Jones' superior officer and partner in Berens River law enforcement, Corporal Hugh Stewart. The next day we had lunch with the latter in his little house.

Neither was very talkative, but the corporal finally told us how he had taken two unruly Crees from Berens River, across the lake to a railway station, and thence to Winnipeg, all alone in the dead of winter. It was a trip of several days.

"Why, how could you sleep?" we asked him.

"Well, I guess I didn't—much," was all he would say about it.

Our ninth story for the *Star* we wrote late at night in the company office, with a mounted policeman on one side, Hudson Bay clerks on the other, and a few trappers and Crees and half-breeds scattered about, watching the curious-looking white boys manipulate a clumsy typewriter by the light of candles. Plenty of inspiration!

Before we went back to our blankets the clerks gave us a block of black pemmican, made from seal meat. As Walt wrote in the story, "It looks like chocolate, smells like limburger cheese, and has a taste all its own." We hid it far down in the grub box.

In our scribbled diary for the next day, the entry begins, "Went over to the log cabin inn. Met Betty Kemp, the owner's daughter."

Betty, our own age, tanned by the Manitoba sun, was a perfect companion for tramping about the settlement and swimming at her own private little beach. Many were the delightful hours we spent dangling our bare legs from a smooth shelf of granite into the cool waters, munching handfuls of rich, fat sand cherries, practically every bush of which Betty had mapped out.

"Won't you go swimming with me tonight?" she asked. "In June I made a vow to take a dip at midnight every night until school begins and I have to go back to Winnipeg. So far I haven't missed once."

At midnight—brrr! It was the twenty-fifth of August and we were about two hundred miles, as the crow flies, north of the Canadian border. And oh, how cold those August nights would get!

"I feel a bad cold coming on," I protested lamely, and shivered once more at the thought of it.

"Don't mind him," Walt told her grandly. "I'd be glad to go with you."

"Very well," I said, "have a good time." But I was thinking, "Don't expect any sympathy from me afterwards and don't expect any more than your share of the blankets, either, you would-be Eskimo."

While I played phonograph records at the inn to keep myself awake, they had their swim under the northern lights. Five minutes after I heard the first splash near the rocks before the inn Walt came into the room, shaking and blue with frost, grabbed a towel, and, between vigorous motions with the cloth, stuttered, "That'll be all f-for m-m-me. Anyway, you snickering hyena. I was b-brave enough t-t-to try it." I drowned out the phonograph with my mirth.

Walt and I had planned to start the stretch of the Lake Winnipeg paddle after his swim that night. Heavy northwest winds forbade all thought of pushing off during the last two days, and Corporal Stewart had suggested we try night traveling for a while, as the turbulent waters seemed to quiet somewhat at sundown.

As we tightened the last strap on our packs, within the inn, one of the men put his hand on my shoulder and said, "Listen."

We were motionless. Then through the trees came the small sound of the sighing wind. Gradually it grew louder, like a siren coming nearer.

With stunning suddenness a storm, a northwestern gale, struck the settlement. The wind howled and the shutters of the inn banged and clattered. Frequent jagged streaks of lightning, followed by thunder which reverberated through the darkened forest, illuminated row upon row of ghastly white billows, far out on the lake, crashing toward the shore. At last all the tales of sudden death on Lake Winnipeg had been confirmed.

The thought of being out there in the canoe made me turn pale.

II

BIG DROPS

RIVERGODS

Richard Bangs and Christian Kallen

Rafting down Chile's famed Rio Bio-Bio.

NO ONE WAS HUNGRY THE next morning, so we skipped breakfast and marched down, a funeral procession, to the first rapid. Jack Morrison, a ten-year Colorado veteran, commented with a grating crack in his voice that this was the first rapid he had seen that was more difficult than Lava Falls on the Colorado—a rapid considered by many to be the toughest piece of whitewater in the United States. After eyeing the stretch in the warming light of morning's optimism, we decided it was just possible to make the run down what we were now calling Lava South. Besides, it would be far preferable to run it than to portage, though the consequences of a mistake could be dear.

Alejandro looked at it and told us he could round up horses to get us out of the canyon. When we didn't respond to his offers, he told us he had two kids, cute with brown eyes, and he elected to walk the rapid.

Bruce rowed first, as Bill and I rode the bow. We pivoted past the tributary waterfall, a grand, miraculous sight, but we couldn't dwell on it. Survival superseded our sense of aesthetics, and all attention was directed downstream.

Bruce made a good entry, but smacked into a lateral wave that turned him the wrong way. The path devised while scouting from shore was the path not taken. We suddenly washed broadside against a boulder bar bisecting the river, and the boat started to ride up on its side, the first stage of a flip. Bill and I threw our weight on the rising tube, and the boat slid off the rock, around the far side into a channel we hadn't been able to see from shore. We were out of control in unknown water. We careened toward a pair of basalt slabs, smashed into one, spun on our side, and flopped down to the rapid's end, right side up. The bilge was brimming with water, and as Bill and I frantically bailed, Bruce pulled to shore on a broken oar. But we made it!

The day continued with a seemingly endless cascade of rapids. At one, Alejandro met a Mapuche Indian who described a recent drowning, and, as it turned out, the victim had been a friend of Alejandro's. At the next rapid, Alejandro explained he had three children, just school age, and again he volunteered to walk.

At another sharp rapid, Jack and George were kicked out of the boat. As Jack was thrown out, his tennis shoe caught on the oarlock, and he ended up dangling helplessly upside-down in the water, dragged along like a stunt man behind a horse. But this was no stunt: he struggled to keep his chin above water and to wrench his shoe free while the boat drifted toward the next cataract, a bad one.

The scene seemed too melodramatic to be real, but a watery scream from Jack dispelled the theatrical illusion. George Wendt splashed back into the bilge, grabbed the oars, and wrested the raft back to shore, while Mike plunged out of the boat next to Jack to help pull the caught leg free. Coughing and spitting, Jack dragged himself up on the beach, a vacant, hurt look in his eyes. He'd come close; it was a freakish close call. Some nasty bruises and a deep cut testified the river couldn't be messed with.

Later that same day Bruce, too, paid his dues. After several cautious, successful runs, Bruce decided to run left through a rapid Jack had already run down the right. It was a mistake.

We suddenly plummeted through space toward a rock at the bottom of a 15-foot hole. We smacked, buckled, twisted, and almost flipped, and Bruce hurtled overboard. I sprang to the oars just as the raft slammed into a cliff. We bounced off, and a few hard pivot strokes spun us into an eddy. No sign of Bruce. A few seconds passed, those steel-cold seconds in which everyone wonders if the worst has happened, then we all broke into a chorus of screams. I felt the floor of the boat bump twice and realized Bruce was stuck underneath. I jumped to the side, about to dive in, when a blue-faced Bruce popped up, alive and sputtering next to the boat.

The day had been too intense to continue any farther. We'd run more big rapids in a single day than are run in twelve days on the Colorado, and a couple were as big as the biggest in the Grand Canyon. We camped across from another 100-foot tributary waterfall, one of dozens that grace this canyon, but we were too weary and jaded to give it proper attention. It was like trying to admire a beautiful painting after having been mugged. We slept in exhaustion, unable to worry about what tomorrow might bring.

The next morning, our sixth on the river, was crisp and clear as a bell. Alejandro went for a hike during breakfast and came back with information some Mapuche Indians had passed on to him. They said there were 23 miles of bad rapids ahead, worse than what we'd been through, including a major waterfall. He'd also heard a rumor that another group had tried to raft the river five years earlier, but they had lined their boats for days down to the first big rapid (which we had hit two days earlier) and there they walked out. Prudent, sane men. He concluded by relating the popular local legend of *chenque*, a cave deep at the bottom of the river where those who drown go. There they live forever, a very good and happy, though perhaps soggy, existence, but they can never resurface.

As was by now the pattern, the morning unrolled a stream of thrilling rapids. At noon, after a surprisingly nasty rapid that we navigated without mishap, we reached a red light. The river pinched into a sliver, barely 50 feet wide, and zigzagged through two tortuous right-angle turns. Most of the water jetted around the first corner, slid down an eight-foot sluice, and crashed into an overhanging cliff on the right. Overhangs—wedges of rock just above the surface—are major risks. Each year they drown a few hapless kayakers and occasionally some rafters. If a boat or body gets swept into an overhang, it easily can get pinned by hundreds of pounds of water pressure, making it impossible to escape.

The overhang ahead of us, coupled with the fact that the next three rapids, all in close succession, were horrendous, gave us pause. We were certain we had now reached the series of difficult rapids we had spotted from the air. From high above, they had all looked runnable. Ground level had a different story to tell. After an hour of scouting through the virtually impenetrable brush and after much deliberation, we decided to portage one boat and position it in the water downstream from the falls. There, we hoped it could catch the other boat, should it capsize.

Alejandro had taken little time to decide to walk out to the road and hitch to Santa Barbara, our takeout point. He felt sure his four hungry children would want to see him again. So Jack Morrison, who had not upset a boat in ten years of river running, started into the rapid with only one crew member. All the others, save Alejandro, were stationed in the other boat below, with coiled safety lines in readied hands.

"Whatever you do, Rich, stay away from that wall," Jack had warned as we pushed off, as if I might skip out of the boat and splash over to the wall for a playful inspection. Still, the tension in his voice put a lump in my throat.

His setup was perfect. He made it all the way to the top left, where the water was safest, but too quickly the current changed and pushed the raft into the right sluice that rammed into the overhang. The wall bore down on us at an alarming speed; I could see the dark recesses of the overhang getting bigger, enveloping the total picture of possibilities. I jumped back, and bam! We hit the wall at a forty-five-degree angle, and the boat ever so slowly slid up the wall, wedged briefly in the overhang, then tipped over. I jumped clear, as did Jack, and we were flushed safely to the eddy below. His first flip—after ten virtuous years of rafting.

Instinctively Jack and I grabbed the D-rings of the boat and tried to drag it to the right shore. It was cumbersome as a pregnant hippo, and I found myself quickly exhausted. We made one small eddy, but couldn't find a handhold or break in the rock to climb out, so we slid back into the current and down around the corner toward the next rapid. The other boat showed in the nick of time and pulled us in barely 25 feet above the angry water. Had we been sucked in, we probably would have lost the boat and gear forever, to say nothing of Jack and myself. Luckily we hadn't sent both boats through the rapid back to back, as we had talked of earlier. The cost would have been high.

This sequence of rapids, each of which was a gamble, was later given the name Royal Flush. The first was the Ace; this second one we called Suicide King. Then we continued through the next rapid, the Queen of Hearts, without mishap; if we hadn't been scared to death, it would have been fun. Shortly thereafter we came to the fourth big one of the day. It was the legendary falls, or *salto*, that the Mapuche had warned us about, and it deserved legendary status. Briefly described, in this rapid—which came to be known as One-Eyed Jack—the river collides with a boulder as big as the Ritz, splits into two channels, then slices, spits, and erupts 15,000 cubic feet of water per second. We decided to portage.

SHIVA WINKED

Tim Cahill

Finding religion on India's Tons River

TWO DAYS LATER, WE HIT
Main Squeeze, the first really nasty rapid. It was hellishly technical. The
river narrowed down to thirty feet, and, naturally, a bridge spanned the
Tons at the point of its greatest fury. The water thundered between rock
walls in wildly irregular waves that clashed, one against the other, throwing spray ten feet into the air. Just before the bridge, the river rose up over
a rock—a domer—then dropped four feet into a hole. The hole was six
feet long, and at its downstream end, a wave four feet high curled back
upstream.

We wanted to hit the hole dead on, power paddle into the curling
wave, punch through, jog right to avoid the tree trunk pylon for the
bridge, duck under the bridge—Jack Morrison said he'd never seen the
Tons so high—then hit hard to the right. Ten feet past the bridge, the
river widened to 50 feet, but a rock 30 feet wide cut the Tons into two 10-
foot channels. The left channel was shallow and rock strewn. We would
need to pull hard right as soon as we passed under the bridge.

There were three boats. Seven of us were in the paddle boat: three of
us on each tube with paddles and Jack Morrison manning the oars from
the frame in the back. Jack called out orders—"paddle right"—and

43

muscled the bow into the line we'd chosen. We had spent two hours scouting Main Squeeze and we ran it smartly in thirty seconds.

Those of us in the paddle boat were getting cocky, impatient with all the scouting Jack thought necessary. We were a strong team and we worked well together. Why couldn't we just R and R: read the river and run? There was some grumbling about this matter.

A tributary I couldn't find on the map—local people called it the Pauer—emptied into the Tons, effectively doubling its volume, just before the town of Tiuni. The river below gathered force and the gradient steepened until the Tons was dropping 100 feet every mile. It was a wild ride, the Tons below Tiuni. There were, for instance, 5 major rapids just below the town, with no more than 20 yards of flat water in the whole run. Occasionally we hit a hole out of position and people were thrown from the boat—"swimmer!"—but we managed to right ourselves and scoop swimmers out of the water without stopping.

A mile downstream from the town, we passed a dozen or so men sitting on the rocks beside a six-foot-high pile of burning sticks. We were paddling hard, dodging rocks, and punching through curlers, but there was time enough to see the body on top of the funeral pyre. A yellow sheet covered the torso to the shins and flames licked at the bare feet.

The ashes would be dumped into the Tons and they'd flow into the Yamuna, which empties into the sacred Ganges. There, in those holy waters, the soul of the departed might achieve *moksha*: liberation from the cycle of being, from the necessity of being reborn.

At the moment, however, the physical body was being consumed in the burning flame of Shiva's open third eye.

On the second to last day, the river entered a long narrow gorge. The cliff walls that rose on either side were an oddly striated travertine that looked like decorations on some alien and inhuman temple. We had come 70 miles, dropped almost 3,000 feet, and the river had spent much of its power. There were long flat-water floats where the river was so quiet we could hear the chatter of monkeys and the calls of cuckoos. The land, which upstream had looked like a steeper version of the northern Rockies, now took on a more gentle, tropical rhythm. Palm trees grew at the edge of the cliffs, and their roots dropped 80 feet into the nourishing water of the Tons.

There were waterfalls here and there, and once, floating languidly under cobalt skies, we passed through a falling curtain of mist that stretched 100 feet along a mossy green cliff wall. It was warmer here, 85 degrees, and I raised my face to the cooling water. The sunlight was scattered in that silver curtain—each drop a prism—so that for a moment what I saw was a falling wall of color that shifted and danced in the breeze. The mist had the scent of orchids in it, and I wondered then why it was that anyone would want to be liberated from the cycle of being.

There was big trouble the last day. The Tons had lately been so flat and friendly that the last series of rapids were a major surprise and are, in fact, called Major Surprise. I followed Jack and his boatmen as they scouted the noisy water: there was a hole, a pretty good curling wave, a house-sized rock, and a small waterfall called a pourover. We needed to skirt the rock, punch through the hole, and pull left in order to hit the pourover at its shallow end, which would give us a drop of about four feet.

Major Surprise ate us alive.

I recall hitting the hole and punching cleanly through the curler. But we didn't get left, not even a little bit, and the boat rose up over a domer so high that I found myself looking directly into the sky. We tipped forward—the drop was eight feet—and the boat seemed to hesitate momentarily, like a roller coaster at the summit of the first rise. This, I told myself, does not bode well.

The first thing a person notices underwater in the turbulence of a big hole is the sound. It's loud: a grinding, growling jackhammer of unrelenting thunder. You do not register temperature and, if you are being Maytagged, you have no idea where you are. It's like catching a big ocean wave a bit low: there's a lot of tumbling involved, not to mention a sense of forces beyond human control.

The river took my swimming trunks. It ripped the tennis shoe off one of my feet, sent me thudding against unseen rocks, shot me to the surface dead center in the middle of the hole, sucked me down again, and batted me around for a period of time I was never able to calibrate. It didn't seem fair. I couldn't even recall falling out of the boat: the entire situation was unacceptable.

Some time later I came to the surface and the hole was behind me. The river ran right, between a large rock and a canyon wall. A person could get wedged in there, underwater. I swam left, and suddenly felt myself being hurtled down a smooth tongue of water toward a series of peaked waves of the type boatmen call haystacks. It was like being sick, like vomiting. After the first painful eruption you think, good, that's all over. But almost instantly your stomach begins to rise—oh, God, not again—and that is the way I felt being sucked breathless into the second rapid.

While I was zipping along underwater, trying to get my feet downstream to ward off rocks, the other members of the paddle boat team were enjoying their own immediate problems and proving Jack Morrison's contention that we were taking the river entirely too lightly. John Rowan and Martha Freeman had been sucked to the right and managed to pull themselves out after the first rapid. Jack and Billy Anderson held on to the boat, which was still stuck in the hole and being battered by the upstream curler wave. Sue Wilson and Douglas Gow were somewhere out ahead of me in the second rapid.

I surfaced and spotted Gow in the flat water between that second and third rapid. He was ten yards downstream and he didn't seem to be swimming at all. His helmet was missing. I thought he might have been Maytagged rather badly, that he might be unconscious, and I am proud to say that I swam to the man who needed help. (Actually, Gow had taken off his helmet because it slipped down over his eyes and he couldn't see.)

"You OK?" I called when I was within arm's reach. Gow practices emergency medicine in Australia and is used to reacting calmly in tense situations. "Fine, thanks," he said, and then—oh, God, not again—I was pulled down into the third rapid.

There was, in time, a sense of water moving more slowly. Sunlight shimmered on the flat-water surface, which seemed to recede even as I swam toward it, but then there was air and a handhold on the rocky canyon wall. Presently, Morrison and Anderson came by in the boat and fished me out of the river. I lay on my belly on the floor of the raft and spit up a quart of yellow water.

We were somewhere else then, pulled up onto the sand at the left side of the river. Sue Wilson and Doug Gow were gasping on the bank. Someone gave me a pair of swimming trunks to wear. This did not seem to be an important matter. I lay on my back, on the floor of the raft, looking at the sun, and there was a moment when it seemed to darken slightly, but I did not lose consciousness. I thought of Shiva's blinding third eye, of a long lewd wink.

DELIVERANCE

James Dickey

The unnerving novel and movie that triggered the nation's interest in whitewater boating

WE MOVED WELL FOR THE better part of an hour. Lewis was keeping up, too, driving the almost-buried canoe forward with an effort I could not even guess at. He liked to take things on himself and, because he could, do more than anyone else. And I was glad to see that in an emergency his self-system didn't fold up on him, but carried on the same, or even stronger.

But I was also very glad that Drew and I were light and maneuverable. There were no rapids, but the river seemed to be moving faster. There was an odd but definite sensation of going downhill in a long curving slant like a ramp. I noticed this more and more, and finally it occurred to me that the feeling was caused by what the land on both sides was doing. At first it had lifted into higher banks, the left higher than the right, and now it was going up raggedly and steadily, higher and higher, changing the sound of the river to include a kind of keep beating noise, the tone coming out more and more as the walls climbed, shedding their trees and all but a few bushes and turning to stone. Most of the time the sides were not vertical, but were very steep, and I knew we would be in real trouble if we spilled. I prayed that there would be no rapids while we were in the gorge, or that they would be easy ones.

We pulled and pulled at the river. Drew was hunched forward in a studious position like a man at a desk, and at every stroke the old GI shirt he wore took a new hold across his shoulders, one which was the old hold as well.

I looked back. We had opened up a little distance on the other canoe; it was about 30 yards behind us. I thought I heard Lewis holler to us, probably to slow down, but the voice, thinly floating through the boom of wall-sound, had no authority and very little being at all.

The walls were at least 150 feet high on both sides of us now. The cross-reverberation seemed to hold us on course as much as the current did; it was part of the same thing—the way we had to move to get through the gorge.

I looked around again, and Lewis and Bobby had gained a little. They were too close to us for running rapids, but there was nothing I could do about it; as far as I was concerned they were going to have to take their chances.

As we cleared each turn, before Drew swung across in front of me I kept looking for white water, and when I'd checked for that I looked along both banks as far downriver as I could see, to try to tell if either of them was lowering. There was no white water, and the walls stayed like they were, gray and scrubby, limestonish, pitted and scabby.

But the sound was changing, getting deeper and more massively frantic and authoritative. It was the old sound, but it was also new, it was a fuller one even than the reverberations off the walls, with their overtones and undertones; it was like a ground-bass that was made of all the sounds of the river we'd heard since we'd been on it. God, God, I thought, I know what it is. If it's a falls we're gone.

The sun fell behind the right side of the gorge, and the shadow of the bank crossed the water so fast that it was like a quick step from one side to the other. The beginning of darkness was thrown over us like a sheet, and in it the water ran even faster, frothing and near-foaming under the canoe. My teeth were chattering; I felt them shaking my skull, as though I had already been in the river and now had to suffer in the stone shade of the bank. We seemed to leap, and then leap from that leap to another down the immense ditch, like flying down an underground stream with the ceiling ripped off.

We couldn't make it to Aintry by dark; I knew that now. And we couldn't survive on the river, even as it was here, without being able to see. The last place I wanted to be was on the river in the gorge in the dark. It might be better to pull over while there was still light and find a flat rock or a sandbar to camp on, or get ready to sleep in the canoes.

We came around one more bend, and at the far end of it the riverbed began to step down. There was a succession of small, rough rapids; I couldn't tell how far they went on. About the only thing I had learned about canoeing was to head into the part of the rapids that seemed to be moving the fastest, where the most white water was. There was not much light left, and I had already made up my mind to get through this stretch of water and pull over to the bank, no matter what Lewis and Bobby decided to do.

The water was throwing us mercilessly. We came out in a short stretch between rapids, but we were going too fast to get out of the middle of the river before the next rocks. I didn't want to risk getting the canoe broadside to the river and then be sucked into the rocks. That would not only spill us, but would probably wedge the canoe on the rocks, and the force of water against it would keep it there. And we couldn't make it downriver with four of us in one canoe, as low in the water and hard to turn as it would be. I tried to hold Drew centered on the white water, to line him up and shoot him through the rocks; if I could get him through, I'd be with him.

"Give me some speed, baby," I hollered.

Drew lifted his paddle and started to dig in long and hard.

Something happened to him. It looked at first—I can see it in my mind in three dimensions and slow motion and stop action—as if something, a puff of wind, but much more definite and concentrated, snatched at some of the hair at the back of his bead. For a second I thought he had just shaken his head, or had been jarred by the canoe in some way I hadn't felt, but at the same instant I saw this happen I felt all control of the canoe go out of it. The river whirled the paddle from Drew's hand as though it had never been there. His right arm shot straight out, and he followed it, turning the whole canoe with him. There was nothing I could do; I rolled with the rest.

In a reflex, just before my head smashed face-first into the white water with the whole river turning around in midair and beginning to swing upside down, I let go the paddle and grabbed for the bow at my feet, for even in panic I knew I would rather have a weapon than the paddle, as dangerous as it would be to have the naked broadheads near me in such water.

The river took me in, and I had the bow. My life jacket brought me up, and Lewis' canoe was on top of me like a whale, rising up on the current. It hit me in the shoulder, driving me down where the rocks swirled like marbles, and something, probably a paddle, thrust into the side of my head as Lewis or Bobby fended me off like a rock. I kicked at the rushing stones and rose up. Downstream, the green canoe drove over the other one broadside, reared nearly straight up, and Bobby and Lewis pitched out on opposite sides. A rock hit me and I felt some necessary thing—a muscle or bone—go in my leg. I kicked back with both feet and caught something solid. I must have been upside down, for there was no air. I opened my eyes but there was nothing to see. I threw my head, hoping I would be throwing it clear of the water, but it did not clear. I was not breathing and was being beaten from all sides, being hit and hit at and brushed by in the most unlikely and unexpected places in my body, rushing forward to be kicked and stomped by everything in the river.

I turned over and over. I rolled, I tried to crawl along the flying bottom. Nothing worked. I was dead. I felt myself fading out into the unbelievable violence and brutality of the river, joining it. This is not such a bad way to go, I thought; maybe I'm already there.

My head came out of the water, and I actually thought of putting it under again. But I got a glimpse of the two canoes, and that interested me enough to keep me alive. They were together, the green one buckled, rolling over and over each other like logs. Something was nailing one of my hands, the left one, to the water. The wooden canoe burst open on a rock and disappeared, and the aluminum one leapt free and went on.

Get your feet forward of you, boy, I said, with my mouth dragging through the current. Get on your back.

I tried, but every time I came up with my feet I hit a rock either with my shins or thighs. I went under again, and faintly I heard what must have been the aluminum canoe banging on the stones, a ringing, distant, beautiful sound.

I got on my back and poured with the river, sliding over the stones like a creature I had always contained but never released. With my life preserver the upper part of my body drew almost no water. If I could get my feet—my heels—over the stones I slid over like a moccasin, feeling the moss flutter lightly against the back of my neck before I cascaded down into the next rapids.

Body-surfing and skidding along, I realized that we could never have got through this stretch in canoes. There were too many rocks, they were too haphazardly jumbled, and the water was too fast; faster and faster. We couldn't have portaged, either, because of the banks, and we couldn't have got out and walked the canoes through. We would have spilled one way or the other, and strangely I was just as glad. Everything told me that the way I was doing it was the only way, and I was doing it.

It was terrifyingly enjoyable, except that I hurt in so many places. The river would shoot me along; I'd see a big boulder looming up, raise my feet and slick over, crash down on my ass in a foaming pool, pick up speed and go on. I got banged on the back of the head a couple of times until I learned to bend forward as I was coming down off the rock, but after that nothing new hurt me.

I was already hurt, I knew. But I was not sure where. My left hand hurt pretty bad, and I was more worried about it than anywhere else, for I couldn't remember having hit it with anything. I held it up and saw that

I had hold of the bow by the broadheads and was getting cut in the palm every time I flinched and grabbed. The bow was also clamped under my left arm, and now I took it out and swung the beads away from me, just before I went over another rock. As I slid down I saw calm water below, through another stretch of rapids: broad calm, then more white water farther down, far off into evening. I relaxed again, not even touching the stones of the passage this time, but riding easily along through the flurrying cold ripples into the calm water, cradling the bow.

I was floating, not flowing anymore. Turning idly in the immense dark bed, I looked up at the gorge side rising and rising. My legs were killing me, but I could kick them both, and, as far as I could tell neither was broken. I lifted my hand from the water; it was nicked and chopped a little in places, but not as badly as it might have been; there was a diagonal cut across the palm, but not a deep one—a long slice.

I floated on, trying to recover enough to think what to do. Finally I started to struggle weakly around to look upstream for the others. My body was heavy and hard to move without the tremendous authority of the rapids to help it and tell it what to do.

Either upstream or down, there was nobody in the river but me. I kept watching the last of the falls, for I had an idea that I might have passed the others, somewhere along. There had probably been several places where the water split and came down through the rocks in different ways; all three of them might be back there somewhere, dead or alive.

As I thought that, Bobby tumbled out of the rapids, rolling over and over on the slick rocks, and then flopped belly-down into the calm. I pointed to the bank and he began feebly to work toward it. So did I.

"Where is Lewis?" I yelled.

He shook his head, and I stopped pulling on the water and turned to wait in midstream.

After a minute or two Lewis came, doubled-up and broken-looking, one hand still holding his paddle and the other on his face, clasping something intolerable. I breaststroked to him and lay beside him in the cold coiling water under the falls. He was writhing and twisting uselessly, caught by something that didn't have hold of me, something that seemed not present.

"Lewis," I said.

"My leg's broke," he gasped. "It feels like it broke off."

The water where we were did not change. "Hold on to me," I said.

He moved his free hand through the river and fixed the fingers into the collar of my slick nylon outfit, and I moved gradually crossways on the water toward the big boulders under the cliff. The dark came on us faster and faster as I hauled on the crossgrain of the current with Lewis' choking weight dragging at my throat.

From where we were the cliff looked something like a gigantic drive-in movie screen waiting for an epic film to begin. I listened for interim music, glancing now and again up the pale curved stone for Victor Mature's stupendous image, wondering where it would appear, or if the whole thing were not now already playing, and I hadn't yet managed to put it together.

As we neared the wall, I saw that there were a few random rocks and a tiny sand beach where we were going to come out; where Bobby was, another rock. I motioned to him, and he unfolded and came to the edge of the water, his hands embarrassing.

He gave me one of them, and I dragged us out. Lewis hopped up onto a huge placid stone, working hard, and then failed and crumpled again. The rock, still warm with the last of the sun that had crossed the river on its way down, held him easily, and I turned him on his back with his hand still over his face.

CANYON

Michael Ghiglieri

A pilgrimage down the dreaded Right Side of Lava Falls

T. A., FABRY, DANNY, AND I perched on the huge block of basalt 30 feet above the tongue of the rapid and stared down at the all-too-familiar chaos of waves pounding over submerged boulders dumped here by those flash floods from the new Prospect Canyon. When I had first stood here to scout this complex rapid in 1976, the flow level had been higher than now, and I had seen no good route through it. The route I finally chose, in ignorance of where other professional guides were running here, was the route called the Dory Slot or the Right Slot. This route had worked even better than I had hoped. For my next dozen trips or so, I stuck to the Slot like glue and polished it like silver. I only started giving serious consideration to alternate routes two years later after a notorious Canyon boatman named Whale said to me, "You haven't run Lava until you've run the Right Side."

I had watched two boats run the Right Side on that first trip. The boatman in boat one ran tandem with me on my first run. Only seconds behind me, he was blasted completely across his boat and into the river like a fly hit by the stream from a garden hose. His boat buckled in two. His aluminum rowing frame bent, then cracked into pieces. As he swam for his life I rowed upstream to intercept him and some of his flotsam. He had confirmed my initial suspicion: the Right Side was for idiots.

I then hiked back up to observe our third boat follow down the Right Side. Maybe, I thought, the trashing of that first boat on the Right Side had been a fluke. I watched. The boat slid off the first diagonal wave, dropped into the V-wave, then bent at right angles. The boatman was knocked off his rowing seat into the bilge in the stern—still gripping both oars by their handles. He struggled there like a turtle on his back, half drowning in two feet of bilge water for what seemed about a minute but was actually only five seconds. Meanwhile, his boat, swamped and out of control, caromed into even bigger waves. Ugly.

But Whale's pronouncement would not stop ringing in my ears, and eventually I arrived at Lava to find the water so low that the Right Side was the only good option. But then it was easy. So I started pushing the envelope on subsequent trips. I studied every nuance in current roaring down that flume of insanity at higher flows, identifying within inches the ideal position for a boat at each critical juncture. Then I started running it.

Whale was right. It was wild. But as the flow levels increased, one's ability to predict one's position and momentum after emerging from the V-wave went down the toilet. I tried slight variations of entry, but at higher flows any finesse was canceled out by the funneling tendency of the V-wave. Still, my good runs far outnumbered my sloppy ones, and I had never gotten into serious danger here. On my last trip we had all run the Right Side and two of us had aced it. I had been half of them.

"I'm gonna run the Right," I announced matter-of-factly. "So I'd like someone to be down there first."

"The Slot's the run," T. A. responded. "It's clean. Why take chances?"

Danny, still uncommitted, stared at the rapid. The Slot was clean, really clean, almost boringly clean, but it required very close attention to navigation. Missing the entry by a foot to the left meant being sucked into the Center Trough and hurting your people. Missing it to the right would automatically funnel the boat into the Right Side but with the wrong momentum and with an almost total lack of control. Danny stared again at the Center Trough and shuddered slightly. The window of opportunity there was so narrow and his performance so far on this trip so sloppy that he decided that the Slot was too risky. And the Right Side was out of the question. "I'm going Left," he finally announced. The Left Side was choppy and sloppy, but since the flood of 1983 had cleared it, it offered a route even at medium flows.

"Who wants to run first?" I asked. We would run this in two groups so our passengers could photograph one another in big water.

"I'll go," T. A. volunteered.

"I'll go, too," Danny said.

Fabry stared at the rapid silently, then said, "I'd like to run second."

I turned to Sutton and Jimbo, our trainees. "Et tu?"

Sutton pondered, then admitted, "Well, I'd like to watch."

Twenty minutes later two boats appeared above the tongue. My heart rate sped up. T. A. ran the Slot and did a nice job of it. Danny ran the Left, and to the relief of his worried passengers, emerged unscathed.

"That didn't look bad," Rowan, one of my passengers, announced. He seemed disappointed. In contrast, his wife, Sheri, stood smiling like a lottery winner and seemed inordinately pleased about the ease of Lava Falls.

"We're going to run it a little differently," I admitted, "on the Right Side. We'll be going for the gusto."

"Good," Rowan approved, perking up. Don nodded in agreement. Tina stood with wrists on hips and head cocked as if to offer an opinion but said nothing. Sheri suddenly appeared crestfallen. Gusto was definitely not on her preferred list. Safety was.

We had stowed the last of our sundry impedimenta, tightened the last strap, and tested every grip line, and I had made sure that my oarlocks were tight in their aluminum sockets. I looked to Fabry.

"Ready?"

He stuck his thumb up and grinned. Jack and Lydia, two Brits sitting in the front of his boat, smiled with him.

"Can you see Jimbo?"

He stood from his rowing seat to peer over a block of basalt in the water, then nodded. "They're ready."

"Have a good run," I offered as I pulled away from shore. He was going for the Slot, Sutton and Jimbo for the Left. We would be the only ones down the Right Side. "Have a good run, Michael," he replied. We both meant it.

As usual above major rapids here, the water was a calm antithesis to what awaited us below the tongue. Its calmness seemed almost accusatory. Choosing the most challenging route in Lava Falls was senseless bravado, this calm water seemed to whisper. I tried to ignore it.

"OK," I started, "we're running the far Right. And, while I don't think we're going to eat it, if anything does happen and you find yourself outside the boat and in the river, swim left with all your might. Don't worry about anything but swimming left—till you are past that huge black rock at the foot of the rapid. Then swim to the right to avoid Son of Lava. Is that clear?"

Sheri and Rowan and Don and Tina were packed hip to hip in a solid phalanx on the front deck. They all nodded. Sheri looked as though she had just swallowed something that had changed its mind.

"Also, I'd like one of you guys to drop forward and wedge yourself in the nose to get your weight up front. Any volunteers?"

"I'll do it," Rowan said immediately. Unlike his wife, he was looking forward to this.

"Great. Thanks. But don't move forward until we're there and I call 'forward.' And as soon as you're there, grab the bowline and the grab line."

"Got you."

Why was I running the Right Side? I asked myself again. Was it because this would be a lot more fun . . . because it was a challenge . . . because Lava Falls was the last really big rapid of the trip? At this water level, 13,000 cubic feet per second, it was the biggest rapid on the entire river. Or was it because you haven't rowed Lava until you've rowed the Right Side? Or was it because this might be my last trip (you never know)?

I knew that this was probably the only trip these people would make here—until their kids grew up.

But was I risking making those kids orphans by running the Right Side? Or my own kids orphans? People had drowned here. I hated this calm float. Why did it have to take so long? But all of those fatalities had been passengers, passengers on motor rigs. No professional Grand Canyon oarsman had been killed here or had lost anyone here. So was I about to make history? What a stupid thought. I reviewed my plan of action and felt my heart rate soar in response to the mental images.

This is ridiculous. I had it easy. I had a top-notch boat under me, tuned to perfection. I knew the route better than most people know their own living rooms. Not everyone had had all of these advantages here.

I thought about James White. He had been dragged sunburned, emaciated, and exhausted from a driftwood raft at Callville, Nevada, on September 8, 1867 (two years before John Wesley Powell's expedition), after what he claimed had been a ten-day float through the most horrendous river canyons known to man. He had been prospecting with two partners in the San Juan Mountains when they had been attacked by Indians and forced to abandon their horses to flee down a tributary canyon of the Colorado. One partner, Captain Baker, was killed by Indians, the second, George Strole, drowned on day four. Two rafts self-destructed, White claimed; the one the friendly Mormons found him clinging to had been his third. Although White claimed for the rest of his long life that he had only run one really bad rapid, a botanist named C. C. Parry, who was attached to a Union Pacific survey party, convinced both White and himself—and the readers of his article in the *Transactions of the St. Louis Academy of Science*—that White had floated the entire Grand Canyon plus Glen Canyon and then some while roped to three or four cottonwood logs.

Had James White really beat Powell by two years? And had he floated through Lava Falls willy-nilly at a flow matching almost exactly this one? Few people think he did—not because it is impossible but because when

White described the canyons and the river to Robert Brewster Stanton 40 years after the journey, he did not describe Grand Canyon or the Colorado as it is here. So where had he been for ten days floating at three miles per hour, fourteen hours per day, a total of 420 miles? From the San Juan River to Callville along the Colorado was roughly 450 miles. Maybe the poor wretch did run Lava on that driftwood raft. Maybe Lava had been his one really bad rapid. If so, what did I have to worry about?

Plenty. But even if White had spent most of his ten days swirling around in eddies and making very slow headway after having launched somewhere on the river at the foot of Grand Canyon a hundred miles downstream from Lava Falls at Pierce Ferry (although how would he have gotten there from the San Juan Mountains?), I had my hands full.

But still it was relatively easy. On Easter Sunday in 1955, Bill Beer and John Daggett arrived at Lee's Ferry to jump into one of the dumbest adventures in the annals of the West. They donned wool long johns, neoprene jackets, life vests, and swim fins, and then grabbed their two big rubber bags of provisions and supplies each and waded into the Colorado. They were planning on *swimming* it, all the way to Pierce Ferry (mile 280). And they did—26 days of near hypothermia. Here at Lava Falls they had no boat, no cottonwood raft, and not much hope either. Staring at this rapid had almost paralyzed them.

"How does it look to you from here?" John shouted to Bill while scouting.

"Worse!"

"Think there's a chance, Bill?"

"What?"

"I say, do you think there's a chance we can swim it?"

"No."

But they had, although mostly underwater. And they survived it. They even had fun. So why worry? Because there were two little kids waiting in Flagstaff for their father, a father trying to extract the last, and the ultimate, essence from this river before losing it.

Suddenly the horizon of Lava Falls rose into view. I had photographed the entire rapid in my mind—a good thing. Because of its drop (reputedly 37 feet but actually only thirteen), we could see none of Lava Falls from here. Now I had to line up for one of the three entries. In seconds, changing my mind would be stupid—or worse.

Pivoting the boat slightly, I lined us up on the left diagonal of the far right tongue. A precision entry was critical. We would glide down this long wave, then slide abruptly over the sharp left diagonal at its end. Once over that, I would plant my right oar and pivot the boat nearly ninety degrees, on a dime, to hit the approaching right diagonal straight on. Once over that wave, we would funnel into the V-wave dead straight. We had to hit it straight.

As I took the first critical stroke, I felt that familiar time-warp sensation. Adrenaline was kicking in, in a big way, and despite all of these landmarks being invisible until the last second, I knew that I could hit each one as accurately as a surveyor with his transit. It did not worry me. I could lead this dance with Lava right up to the V-wave. It was what might happen in the V-wave—and immediately afterward—that really worried me.

"OK, Rowan, get forward!"

A space suddenly gaped on the front deck. Hips slid together to fill it.

"OK, hold on!"

Splash. The Domar bucked over the lower left diagonal. I pivoted. We splashed harder into the right diagonal. We were on track. The V-wave yawned before us like the entrance to a tunnel of love that had suddenly switched to the dark side.

Why the Right Side? echoed again in the back of my head. Shut up.

"Lean forward and hold on!" I hunched forward in the rowing seat, pressed my calves against the side boxes to wedge myself, and held my oar handles in a death grip.

Sploosh! We all vanished under water. "Come out straight," I commanded the boat.

"Oh shit!" I heard myself swear. The V-wave had belched us out toward the right shore. Even worse, it had shoved us there stern first. To get us out of trouble, I had to row us left. Dead ahead was the huge, infamous black boulder of lava, Dead Man's Rock, interrupting the flow on which we were now trapped. That rock had destroyed several boats beyond recognition. In five seconds we would be there. But with my stern to the right wall I could not push this boat swamped with two tons of water to the left. Nor did I have time to pivot the necessary 180 degrees. Polished columns of basalt raced past us almost within touching distance. The lava monolith ahead grew as if someone were magnifying it with a zoom lens. I pushed on my oars to the left and felt a surge shove us back even farther right.

When Sheri heard "Oh shit!" she knew it was over. This was not her first river; Rowan and she had done many. But their last experience on the Youghiogheny had almost killed her. They had lain awake most of the night before for ten rainy hours in a leaky tent. Because the rain never stopped, they expected the outfitter to cancel and give them a rain check. But no, the trip was on. Two couples to a boat—and with no guide on board. Directions at critical rapids would be yelled to them. After hours of drizzle they entered the most critical rapid, zigged when they should have zagged, hit a rock, flipped their boat, and all four of them had ended up in the dark, icy womb of a giant washing machine under the boat. Sheri was five months' pregnant. The wild water and darkness became a nightmare. She hit bottom and swallowed a week's ration of water. Before Rowan finally shoved the boat aside, Sheri had resigned herself to dying with her unborn child. Eventually she felt Rowan tugging her to shore. And she thought she might live. But with no sun they got colder and colder until hypothermia set in. It had been a nightmare. But it had been small potatoes on a trivial little river. This was the Right Side of Lava Falls on the mighty Colorado . . . and the guide was saying, "Oh shit!"

But everyone else was having a great time. Ignorance is bliss. It was wild out here, like jumping into the screen during a disaster movie.

Almost everyone else. I was not happy with the current turn of events either. I shoved again on the oars, hoping against hope for lateral gravity slop to edge us left. Grasping at straws. I pulled on the right oar to straighten us for the inevitable collision with that black monolith that had caught hundreds and hundreds of boats, absolutely destroying some of them.

En route, we plunged through two more huge waves and troughs, each of them burying us so deep that we had to hold our breath.

The black rock ahead now seemed the right size for King Kong's throne.

"High side and hold on!" I yelled.

Feverishly, I pulled one last stroke on the right oar, pushed on the left, and got the boat to straighten out. The mammoth collision of the river with that rock surged us up so high that, for an instant, I could see over the top of it to the other boats waiting in the eddy below. I saw eyes in circles of surprise.

Miraculously, the surge subsided and we went with it. I never even felt the slight bump that would have come had the boat touched the rock. The current swished us around the monolith and into the haystacks of the tail waves. Relief washed over me like nothing in Lava Falls had. "Whew," I heard myself utter as I pivoted to pull into that eddy. Luck of the Irish.

Close. Very close.

Everyone spun on the front deck and cheered. No one who has ever won an Academy Award could have faked greater elation. Rowan effused, "That was a great ride! A great ride!"

I smiled weakly. It was as if the hangman coming for me had just tripped, stumbled, fallen through his own trap door, and hanged himself.

Rowan asked, "Can we go back and do it again?"

The answer to the question, Why the Right Side of Lava? was pretty obvious now.

Because it was fun.

RUNNING THE AMAZON

Joe Kane

The only expedition to successfully navigate the entire length of the Amazon

BELOW US LAY THREE BAD
rapids, a short stretch of calm water, and then, where the gorge suddenly
narrowed, a single, 20-foot-wide chute through which the whole frustrated Apurimac poured in unheeding rage. The river was whipped so
white over the next half-mile that it looked like a snowfield. The thrashing
cascades raised a dense mist, rendering the dark canyon cold and clammy.
Their roar made my head ache.

"You swim in that," Bzdak shouted in my ear, "you don't get out!"

But the gorge walls were nearly vertical. We could not portage, we
could not climb out, we could not pitch camp. Even had we found a
relatively flat area, as the gorge cooled through the night boulders would
pop out of the ramparts. The rock shower would be deadly.

We had no choice but to attempt to "line" the raft, a tedious, nerve-
racking procedure in which we sent the raft downriver unmanned at the
end of Chmielinski's 150-foot climbing rope a length at a time.

While I stood on a boulder on the left bank and held the Riken in place
by a short, thin line tied to its stern, the two Poles affixed the heavy
climbing rope to the bow and worked downstream with it as far as they
could. At Chmielinski's signal I dropped my line and kicked the raft into

the first rapid. Within seconds the boat was hurtling through the rapid at what must have been 20 knots, leaping wildly. I shuddered when I imagined riding it.

In the middle of the second rapid, the raft flipped. As it passed the Poles, half the bow line snagged underwater, tautened, and though rated with an "impact force" of more than a ton snapped as if it were mere sewing thread.

Unleashed, the raft sped down the river.

Truran, who had run the first rapid in his kayak, was waiting on a boulder near the calm water above the terrible chute. When he saw the raft break free, he dove into the river, swam for the raft as it drifted toward the chute, and managed briefly to deflect it from its course. He scrambled aboard, and as the raft accelerated toward the chute he caught a rescue line thrown like a football by Chmielinski. The Pole arrested the raft as it teetered on the chute's lip, and slowly hauled Truran back from the edge of disaster. (Chmielinski later described Truran's effort as one of the bravest he had seen on a river.)

Draining as all that was, we still had to get the boat through the chute, somehow hold it to the wall and board it, and then run the ugly water below. The lower rapid could not be scouted. We could only hope that it held no surprises—no waterfalls, no deadly holes.

Jourgensen and Van Heerden slowly worked their way down to the chute, creeping along the boulders that sat at the foot of the gorge's left wall. When they arrived, Chmielinski told them to rest. Then he and Truran anchored the raft with the stern line while Bzdak took the bow line, now shorter by some forty feet, and climbed hand over hand up the two-story boulder that formed the chute's left gate. From the boulder Bzdak then climbed to a footwide ledge that ran along the left wall.

At Chmielinski's command I followed Bzdak. I ascended the boulder easily enough, but negotiating the wet, slick wall was something else. It was so sheer that I couldn't find a solid grip, and I quickly developed what rock climbers call "sewing-machine legs," an uncontrollable, fear-induced, pistonlike shaking. I felt cut off and alone. One misstep and I was in the river, which now churned angrily 15 feet straight below.

Bzdak stopped on the ledge three feet in front of me and looked back. He shouted to me, but I couldn't hear him above the river's tumult. He inched his way back and put his head next to mine.

"DON'T LOOK DOWN!"

We wormed along the ledge until we could lower ourselves onto a one-foot-square rock at the base of the wall and a few feet in front of the gate boulder. We squeezed onto that small rock, each of us with one foot on it and one in the air, and braced ourselves as best we could, trying all the while to ignore the exploding river next to us.

Bzdak twirled the climbing rope up off the top of the gate boulder and tugged on it, signaling Chmielinski to send the raft. I wrapped my arms around Bzdak's waist and leaned back like a counterweight. The raft vaulted the chute. Hand over hand, Bzdak reeled in slack line as fast as he could. I tensed, anticipating the jolt we were about to receive. The raft approached us, shot past, and BOOM! the line straightened and stretched, the raft hurtled down the rapid, I tried to calibrate my backward lean—

"HOLD ME, JOSE!"

I couldn't. We were going in.

Yet somehow Bzdak was hauling the raft toward us, fighting it home inch by inch. Then the line was in my hands and he was in the raft, tearing a paddle loose from beneath the center net. The raft smashed up against the left wall. The river pounded through the chute, curled into the raft, knocked Bzdak flat, and buried him.

Trying to hold the raft was like pulling against a tractor. I couldn't do it. But the raft bailed itself quickly, and Bzdak rose from the floor and paddled toward the rock. When he was five feet away he leapt for it. How he managed to land on that tiny space I do not know, but we made our stand there, anchoring the bucking raft from what seemed like the head of a pin.

We watched Van Heerden help a ghost-white Jourgensen over the boulder and along the wall, then down the wall into the raft. The two men took up positions in the front of the raft. Then Chmielinski climbed over the gate boulder with . . .

. . . I read Bzdak's lips: "Shit!" . . .

. . . Odendaal's kayak.

Its owner appeared behind Chmielinski and stared at us. Chmielinski took aim and shoved the kayak down the boulder's face, dead on into the center of the lurching raft. Then he signaled me into the raft, but the rope had sawed my hands to bloody pulp and I couldn't uncurl them. Bzdak shook the rope loose. I dove the five feet from the wall to the raft and crawled to the left rear. Chmielinski worked his way down the wall and took Bzdak's spot. Bzdak jumped into the raft. With Jourgensen squeezed between them, he and Van Heerden got their paddles ready on front. I reached beneath the center net and yanked out a paddle for me and one for Chmielinski.

"What are we doing?" I yelled to Chmielinski.

He yelled back, "Francois goes alone, he dies!"

Biggs and Truran had managed to traverse the river above the chute and sneak down the far side of the rapid, but it was too risky for Odendaal. Were he to make a single mistake during the traverse he would plunge through the chute and into what we could now see was a deadly hole a few feet below it. Instead, Chmielinski intended to mount Odendaal and his kayak on the raft and run the rapid.

Chmielinski had tried that strategy with an overwhelmed kayaker once before, in the Colca canyon. Like Odendaal's, that kayak had been almost as long as the raft, and with it strapped over the center net the wildly top-heavy raft had flipped moments after it entered the rapid. Everyone had taken a bad swim, Bzdak the worst of his life. If that happened here, we would drown in the hole. But Chmielinski reasoned that it was better that six men risk their lives than that one be condemned to a near-certain death.

I looked up at Odendaal, standing atop the boulder. His eyes were frozen. He looked paralyzed. I knew the feeling.

Chmielinski screamed at Odendaal. He inched his way to the raft and into it and mounted himself spread-eagled on top of his kayak, facing to the rear.

"Squeeze on that kayak like it is your life!" Chmielinski yelled.

Chmielinski could not hold Odendaal's added weight. He leapt and landed in the raft as it bucked away from the wall. Seconds later, even before I could thrust Chmielinski's paddle at him, we were sucked into the heart of the current. With Chmielinski screaming at the top of his lungs "LEFT, LEFT, LEFT!" we managed to turn hard and get the nose of the boat heading downstream. We skirted the ugly hole, but it shoved the raft sideways. We found ourselves bearing down on a "stopper" rock no one had seen, a rock that would upend us if we hit it.

Chmielinski screamed "RIGHT, RIGHT, RIGHT!" and we were sideways, then "IN, IN, IN!," a steering command intended for me, and I hung far to my left and chopped down into the water and pulled my paddle straight in toward me so the rear end of the boat swung left and the front end right. Then a wall of water engulfed me and all I saw was white.

Somehow we shot around the stopper rock's left side but we were still sideways in the rapid "GO, GO, GO, GO!" paddling hard forward fighting in vain for control and the river slammed us up against another rock, this one sloping toward us, Chmielinski's side of the raft shot up on the rock, mine lowered to the river coming behind us, the water punched at the low end, drove it into the rock and stood the raft up on its side, teetering, "UP, UP, UP, UP, UP!" and I fought to climb the high side, to push it back down with my weight, but Odendaal and his kayak had me blocked and I saw Bzdak trapped the same way on the front end, the water pouring in knocked me off my feet, the boat started to flip "GO, GO, GO, GO!" and all I could do was try to paddle free of the rock digging blindly with my paddle "GO, GO, GO, GO!" and BOOM! we were free and bouncing off the left gorge wall and then heading straight for the gentle tail at the end of the rapid and the calm flat water beyond.

KAYAKING THE FULL MOON

Steve Chapple

A colorful encounter with the rapids of the Yellowstone River

WE PLANNED TO SCOUT THE canyon in a rubber raft before making the descent by kayak. Strobel arrived late, something about a fight with his girlfriend on the way to the airport, but he brought a small, 13-foot commercial-grade raft fitted with an aluminum rowing frame. Dave was familiar with Yankee Jim, but to be even safer, we had hired Rowdy Nelson, a 21-year-old local water man who for several summers had rowed the canyon for the Chico rafting company. By the end of the summer, the river had gotten too low and dangerous for commercial rafting, and Rowdy was now free.

We drove five miles to the head of the canyon and suited up. Dave discovered he had forgotten the pump. We spent two hours driving to Gardiner and visiting the bars that were open for the morning trade (which was every one: K-Bar, Blue Goose, and Town) until we found a chipper, bearded river rat with a Rainier longneck in front of him who was willing to loan us the proper pump.

I was annoyed by the delay, but Dave and Rowdy are not the sort of people who become annoyed. Rowdy was a handsome character of near-movie star looks who wore open river sandals, neon surfing fashions, and shorts from Bali. Like Strobel, he was a very calm person. Nothing fazed him. I was beginning to realize that wild rivers did not necessarily attract wild people, but rather the opposite: calm people who at heart do not wish to be calm and are in search of the edge that danger brings.

Rowdy was from an old Montana family in the Paradise Valley, south of Livingston. His grandmother had recently sold their ranch on Deep Creek to Jeff Bridges, the actor, and though Rowdy considered Bridges "a good man," he seemed a bit unsettled by what had happened. Now he guided the river in the summer and planned to move in the fall to Whitefish, near Glacier National Park, where he would teach skiing.

Like Strobel, Rowdy is an artist on the river. Yankee Jim Canyon begins like a horror movie, deceptively nice, a flat stretch, birds chirping. But as you travel down that first half-mile of flat water, you can't help but notice that the river drops like an amusement park ride. You cannot see the rapids just around the first bend, but as you approach, you hear them, louder and louder. It's like the start of a roller coaster where you pull slowly up the track, knowing all along what must happen after you reach the top.

This first rapid is called Boat Eater. With the sad, slight smile he always wore, Rowdy explained that "you had to be a little careful with Boat Eater." Earlier in the summer his boss had been rowing a group of tourists. The man made the wrong approach. The long raft flipped. The tourists had had to swim for it. A nine-year-old boy was unable to make it to shore. They fished him out below Carbella, "kinda shaken."

I once bought some land in the Beartooths from a man who entered Yankee Jim with two customers in a johnboat, which is a flathulled, square-backed dinghy. The johnboat capsized at the start of the canyon, which would have been where we were, and only the man who sold me the land survived. I remembered what the mechanic at the Paradise Flying Service had said after Duane's Cessna touched down and we were talking about our reasons for returning to Montana. "Buddy of mine drowned there last month. They were in a Mackenzie drifter, fishing. Stupid thing to do, a Mackenzie in Yankee Jim." The big mechanic wiped his hands on an oil rag, and shrugged.

I was glad we had hired Rowdy because he looked like a kid who rarely did stupid things, at least when he wasn't on his own time. For control, Rowdy rowed backward. The current snapped and rose all around us. Only a few times did water wash over the transom or slap us in the face, but that was because Rowdy was good. It was not at all hard to imagine how folks who were not so good might get wet, in a different type of boat.

The next rapid is called Big Rock. "Try to avoid that one, OK?" said Rowdy, methodically pulling away from the suck. "If you can help it."

We looked back. Dave, who had been following in his yellow Prijon, was surfing Big Rock. The eddy is so strong that it crashes back upstream, and it's a lot of fun (if you are someone like Dave) to trap yourself in its queasy hole and ride the reverse wave upstream. Big Rock is a perpetual wave machine. A body can surf it forever, since the downstream current holds you in place, if you are good.

Dave noticed that we were looking at him. He took his Harmony black graphite paddle and tossed it a few feet into the air like a majorette at halftime. This meant the only way for him to keep the kayak from capsizing was to hold it with hip action alone, which he did, as white water splashed over him to the top of his helmet, on both sides at once, and also from the front, over the rock, at which point the five-foot paddle came down perfectly into his hands, and he pivoted to join us at the approach to Boxcar.

The train for which Boxcar Rapids is named is supposedly at the bottom, pinned by the boulders fifty feet down. The train spilled late one night in the last century when Yankee Jim was soused.

Boxcar is not a single problem but a long run of soup. If there were sandy beaches on both sides, kayaking there would look like fun—if you capsized, you could swim to the banks. But at this point in the canyon, the waves are inverted. They don't rise up. They rise down, like a stone pyramid stood on its head, on both sides. If you lose your boat, there is nothing to hold on to. You must swim, keeping to the center of the current, which is the strongest and most difficult part, for a mile or so. If you are brushed toward the rock wall, you will be sucked under.

"But if you have a life preserver?" the Brazilian asked Rowdy.

"The state requires 'em," Rowdy shrugged. "Probably better to be a strong swimmer, here."

About two-thirds of the way down the run there is a massive, sloping rock that is not as steep as the walls. We gave it an ironic, placid name: Picnic Rock. There was a C-2 canoe with a bashed prow wedged in a crevice of Picnic Rock. Up on the rock was a man in a bikini bathing suit. His knees and nose were bleeding.

"Y'OK?" shouted Rowdy.

The current was fast. Dave was now alongside the man in his elegant covered canoe. The man waved us off. He said something in German. In a second, in a hairpin cove a hundred yards downstream, was another C-2 full of Germans, a woman and a man, both wearing bikinis.

"Need help?" Rowdy shouted.

"No, no!" the man answered.

We looked upstream. Strobel was paddling backward, for the challenge. The first German was still bleeding, resting. The current tugged the sea rudder at the end of his C-2, threatening to whip the boat off Picnic Rock and back into the river.

Dave shot alongside us.

"Don't think they knew what they were in for," said Rowdy.

"Don't think so," agreed Dave.

I didn't sleep well that night. Around four, I scissored my body out of the folding twin bed and opened the trailer door. I stared out at the wide spot in the Yellowstone where Strobel had tried to teach us a few things. In that pellucid light, all the furniture of our little world was in focus: single cottonwoods scattered like palms, the line of willows at river's edge, river, swirl of river's eddies, and beyond, the flowing hummocks of lava, covered these millions of years by bunch and yellow gamma grass, and long beyond, still higher, the granite escarpment that stands like a jagged wall in front of Dog Tooth Rock, which rose as the last thing I could see to the west, closing off the night sky, a volcanic cone powdered with summer snow, reflecting back a pale fishbelly white in the Montana moon. It was as if I were looking through a camera lens.

I felt a distanced clarity. Behind on Red Mountain, the coyotes were with me, again, I noticed, and that made me smile. Coyotes are basically small wolves, and I made a mental note to check out the wolf farm that now existed above Paradise Valley, downriver. The government planned to reintroduce wolves to Yellowstone Park. Sheep and cattle ranchers were beginning to raise a cry, but what I wondered right then was, how would the coyotes take the news? They would be like little brothers who had had the run of the family farm for a long, long time, about 110 years, ever since the government had stopped paying a major bounty for wolf ears (around $15 in 1911), and now big brother was coming home, and big brother wolf was more of a taker than a sharer. The coyotes yipped on, unsuspecting.

Finally I scanned the canyon through the delicate arch of Carbella's iron bridge. It was almost dawn. I heard the door of the van open. It was my sister, fully dressed. She did not see me. I watched. Persis picked her way through the sage and scattered cactus to the river, and then, as I had, she stared long upstream, at the dark granite mouth of Yankee Jim. She was still staring when I softly closed the door.

We started at ten. Yankee Jim Canyon in kayaks was not the piece of cake Strobel had predicted, but it was almost the same thing, a piece of fear, since in our kayaks the journey was over so quickly you would have had to have learned nothing at all to have had time to be afraid.

What makes you feel so good on a run like Yankee Jim is that you must concentrate. You are forced to lash mind and body together. No time to think, worry, whine, plan, cavil, or speculate on anything that isn't about to hit you in the face or wash over the kayak's bow within 60 seconds, and that's stretching it.

I did not dare look to the left or to the right, but I still saw the inverted black granite walls flash by like curtains. The boat jumped up and down and I took shotgun shots of water in the face, but the point was to stay in the center of the current and away from the canyon walls. Staying dry at the edges was the mistake. It is a very powerful river, the upper Yellowstone. I enjoyed it.

At the end of the three major rapids is a flat run. Here an osprey hovered over three merganser ducks. There must have been some small fish beneath the ducks; I don't know that osprey prey on other birds. All four rose up as I crashed through. This reminded me of a time long ago when I was a child visiting San Francisco. My brother had been mustered out of Korea, alive, and the parents drove down from Montana to celebrate at the St. Francis Hotel, which fronts on Union Square. I liked to cross the street to the square and run through the crowds of pigeons that rose off the park like clouds of white handkerchiefs. For someone six years old, this was a feeling of strange power. And then I understood I must be safe on the river, because I was no longer concentrating on what I had to do in the present. And then I passed under the elegant metal bridge high above my helmet, and then came our campsite, and my family, who screamed from the bank.

My sister is very macho. Not so macho that she did not want to run the canyon without Strobel behind her but macho enough to want to push the current a bit. She made it through Boat Eater, but she decided to surf Big Rock as she had seen Strobel do behind me. Her kayak flipped. Persis flipped back, tried to roll, once, twice, but she was still mostly underwater. Strobel streaked toward her, his first piece of real work since we had hired him. But Persis was head to the sky by the time Strobel drew alongside, paddling furiously downstream out of anger at her mistake and also at what she saw as her overreaching ambition, I think. By that time, I had gotten out of my boat, and Ines and I could see from the cliff what had happened, but Persis never mentioned it, and Strobel had the sense to keep quiet, too. In my family, at least with the women, middle age seems to come late, if it is acknowledged at all, and at sixty-one Persis may have been entering a mid-life crisis. I only hoped I would live that long.

RIVER

Colin Fletcher

A contemplative descent down Cataract Canyon

THE WHOLE SEQUENCE WENT like clockwork. Particularly Capsize Rapid. Halfway down, pulling hard, I looked over my shoulder at precisely the right moment and immediately saw my rounded-rock marker on the barrier line of white water. I Powelled through dead on target. The relatively slack water beyond gave me even more time than I'd expected to pivot the bow so that it faced new bankside dangers. Adjust onto planned line. Ferry on down, under absolute control. Let bow brush, exactly as intended, a triangular-rock marker. Then, as I straightened out to run a final tongue down into the clear—even before we entered the tongue, because I knew we would hit it dead center—I laughed and shouted out loud, "Perfect!"

The elation still swirled as I threaded us through the rest of Mile-Long with the confidence of a pro who'd been at it for years.

Now, confidence can slither undetected into overconfidence. And hubris spells danger.

Just before either Rapid 18 or 19—I'm not sure which, because I hadn't bothered to check the guide—the full flow of the river, confined and swift but without white water, swung across at an angle from the right wall to left. In mid-swing it divided on each side of a huge boulder and dropped away in two smooth tongues. I could see the far tongue, left of the boulder, clear down to the place it leveled off into flat water. Without much thought, I chose the shorter route, right of the boulder, and floated languidly toward it—broadside on, bow left, ready to make minor adjustments to avoid any obstacles in the short stretch of it that lay out of my sight. I was almost at the drop-off when I saw, over the raft's right tube, that this tongue did not, like the other, glide serenely down into the flat water. It poured over into a horrendous hole that spanned the tongue's entire width.

No time to pivot, then pull left. So I pushed, frantically, both oars. The imminent glassy lip of the drop-off and the seething maw below, now all too visible, goaded me on. Inch by inch we began to ease left, toward the big boulder—away from the lip, from the hole. Very slowly, we gained momentum. For a moment I thought we were going to be swept up onto the boulder and jam solid. But then we'd lifted onto the bulge of water above the boulder's sloping base. We hung there, almost motionless. Then we were sliding down into the safety of the far tongue.

Minutes later I pulled ashore above Rapid 20. The adrenaline was ebbing, fast. Suddenly I felt drained.

Dave Stimson had drawn my attention to Rapid 20 but had remained vague. When I asked for specifics, he smiled and said, "The guide rates it '1,' but . . . Well, you'll see." (The river guide rated each rapid on a scale of 1 to 10. Capsize was a 6; Lower Big Drop, 10.) By now I'd learned to appreciate the way Dave metered his advice: enough information to post warnings and plant signposts, not enough to tarnish expectation; plenty of latitude for me to deal with details. For Rapid 20, he'd left me wondering.

My first impression: a confusion of black boulders and white water. No hint of a route. Second impression: ditto.

By now it was nearly three o'clock. Lunch long overdue. I lunched, siestaed. Afterward, though, even wearier. No doubt now: the disturbed night had caught up with me.

I did walk slowly down and scout the rapid. Close up, it looked horrific. Mostly, a confusion of whitewater obstacles. At its foot, a curving drop-off that blocked all except a narrow channel, left. This channel guarded by a large boulder and its godawful hole.

I dragged myself back up to the raft. I'd meant to camp that night just above Lower Big Drop. But by now I'd grasped that it was stupid and dangerous to run a "bad" rapid when you were operating at anything short of peak performance. Besides, by morning light the run might look easier. So I camped where I'd pulled in.

Afternoon eased into evening. After dinner I leaned back against my dry-bag backrest. The food had injected enough energy for a reassessment.

All along, I'd known that Cataract posed a test. A test that would last little more than a day but would scan my fitness for the month-long run of the Grand Canyon. And ahead, now, lay Cataract's cusp. In the next two miles the river dropped 72 vertical feet—and climaxed in the cusp's cusp: Lower Big Drop. Yet for the moment I felt more nervous about this next rapid.

Briefly, I scouted the lining possibilities. But my heart wasn't in it. I had to run this one. If I balked, how could I pretend to be ready for Lower Big Drop, let alone Crystal and Lava Falls in Grand Canyon? (By now, I guess, I'd fully embraced, almost without further thought, the idea that I'd try to run all the river's rapids.)

Dusk deepened. Downriver, the canyon's irregular and crumbly red walls were sinking toward gray. "The attraction of Cataract," Dave Stimson had said, "is the rapids, not the rock."

I closed my eyes. Well, all right, I'd scout Rapid 20 again in the morning. And probably run it.

Close below me, the rapid roared something like defiance. I listened more intently.

No, it didn't really roar: this one didn't intimidate with size. It snarled: its threat lay in confusion. But if you failed to sort out the confusion—to dampen the "noise" in its communication sense—and found yourself down at the foot, heading inexorably for that line of holes . . .

I comforted myself with two warring quotes. First, somebody's insight that "life is not a gift but an open-ended loan, liable to be called without notice at fate's whim." Then Nietzsche's edict: "That which doesn't kill you makes you stronger." You had to stomach the Nietzschean machismo and allow the underlying truth. Had to allow that facing physical danger can help raise you up from a condition in which you look out on a bleak world and ask plaintively, "Is this all there is?" Can help lift you back on track and leave you gushing, "Oh, what a wonderful life!" Can help you, that is, to achieve just the kind of alchemy that long journeys are—whether you know it or not—often designed to engender.

I reopened my eyes. Downriver, the canyon walls had faded to ghost spaces. Overhead, a star-spangled wedge of night sky.

Now, I'm reasonably accustomed to facing physical dangers. Dangers keen enough to threaten life. And I've always accepted them. But sitting there at the head of Rapid 20 I found myself accepting in a new way. I was aware that the next mile, the next 200 miles, would strain my sketchy rafting capabilities to their limit. Aware that if things went wrong, down at the foot of Rapid 20, for example, and I flipped, out here on my own, with heavy water below, then I might not make it. And I found myself accepting that possibility in a new way. Looking back, I was no longer sure that in the past I'd done so. Not sure I'd faced the reality head-on, eyes open. But this time I felt I did accept. Did so with a certain stoicism. Stoicism of a new kind. I seemed to say to myself, "I've had a good life. And if this is it . . . well, all right."

Night displaced dusk. Down to my right, the rapid snarled on.

Mind you, I wasn't sure I trusted myself. My conversion probably went no more than intellect-deep. If things went wrong I'd fight like hell against extinction. After all, that was how we organisms are constructed. How we have to be constructed.

Next morning, after a good night's sleep, back to the nitty-gritty.

By morning light the run at first looked no easier. But a lengthy scout disclosed a possible way through. When I pushed out into the current, post-Emmett, semi-confidence ruled.

Halfway down the rapid. Ferrying bow right. Still on the chosen line. And the water ahead looking rather less fierce than I'd feared . . . Then we were not on line but being pulled right. Being drawn toward the line of holes across the foot of the rapid. Pull hard, both oars. Pull like mad. At first, no change. Then—painfully slowly—inching back toward the line that meant safety. Moments later we eased in behind and below the big boulder and its godawful hole. Now ferry in close to the left bank, then spin the bow downriver. Done. We went through the narrow channel dead center, comfortably clear of the line of holes, and slowed into quiet water.

Rapids 21 and 22—Upper and Middle Big Drop, both rated 7—were big water but fairly straightforward. (Though Middle Big Drop at high water is apparently "a terrifying, gigantic river-wide wave that's unavoidable.") No serious problems. As soon as we emerged from Middle Big Drop, I looked ahead. Not far below, the river vanished. Just ended. As if cut off. With a knife.

III

THE FAR NORTH

DANGEROUS RIVER

R.M. Patterson

A classic journey by an early pioneer down Canada's Nahanni River

THE NAHANNI WAS QUIET here: no sound came from it except sometimes a gentle lapping of the water on the stones. As one looked upstream, northwest into the canyon, the river swung to the right and disappeared between the towering walls. Two big cottonwoods close by the cabins had just been felled by the beavers; the chips could not be more than a day old; some of the tender shoots had been eaten and some of the bark gnawed off the branches. It was late in the afternoon now, and the shadow of the great cliff above the Hot Springs was creeping across the river towards the old cabins: there was a faint blue haze, perhaps of smoke, in the air, and the edge of the shadow was visible in the haze. Thousands of wildly gyrating bugs danced in the warm, still air. They danced most thickly, or so it seemed, along the shadowline—whirling pinpoints of silver light in the sunshine, vanishing utterly as they passed into the shadow of the canyon wall.

The beach down by the canoe was tramped and churned as if all the moose on the Nahanni had yarded there. As I shoved the canoe out into the current a stone rolled with a clatter on the far shore: I looked up and saw a bull moose walk down to the river to drink, just above the sulphur stream. I have passed the Hot Springs 11 times since then and camped there for several days, but always, when I think of the place, I see the picture of that first afternoon with its hummingbirds and columbines, the bugs, the bull moose, and the beaver cuttings.

I poled the canoe on into the shadows, and it was not long before I was in the water up to my waist hauling the canoe "by the snoot," as Faille called it, up Lafferty's Riffle. This riffle—the second strongest in the Lower Canyon—had, in those days, built up for itself a great, crescent-shaped bar of shingle reaching halfway across the river. The main stream flowed round the end of the bar and roared down the steep drop, foaming and bellowing under the cliffs. The rest of the river had cut channels for itself through the bar and the water raced down these in swift, brawling chutes, each one strong enough to sweep a man off his legs and most of them too deep to wade. I had not met anything like this before, and I had not yet developed the "bar technique" that I built up later from experience. The affair at Lafferty's Riffle that last evening of July was simply a brute, head-on collision between me and the Nahanni. All I brought to the contest was a certain inborn river sense and an ability to see what water was going to do with a canoe before it had done it. Using this and the experience gained in The Splits, I reached the head of the riffle after a hard struggle—soaked but victorious. The riffle had changed greatly when I saw it 24 years later, in 1951: it had become a much simpler affair, a straight hill of water.

The river made a sharp turn to the left (as one faced upstream) and in the middle of the next reach was a bar of sand and shingle with plenty of driftwood lying about on it. There I made camp, and very soon a fire was blazing on the sand, a few wet rags of clothing dangled from the roots of stranded trees, and I was warm and comfortable in old cord riding trousers, heavy shirt, and sweater. The last rays of the sun went off this east-west reach as I was having supper, and I soon found myself reaching for a mackinaw jacket. The contrast, in one week's travel, between this canyon world of cool breezes and cold, rushing waters and the sweaty, mosquito-infested plain of the Liard was almost unbelievable.

After supper I walked up to the head of this shingle island. At the upper end of the reach the river swung sharply to the right, or north, so that in every direction—upstream, downstream, and on either shore—one was faced with the tremendous canyon walls. They rose sheer from the talus slopes at their feet, with mosses and dwarf firs growing on the ledges: limestone and sandstone they were, in level strata, but the colors of the rocks were fading now and the cliffs were turning blue in the twilight. From all sides came the noises of swift, clashing water.

Never in my wildest dreams had I hoped to see anything like this. Away in the distance, at the foot of the island, the tiny flame of the campfire could be seen, flickering and winking: wreaths of blue wood smoke from it were drifting away down the canyon. Somewhere I had seen something for which this wild scene might have been the prototype: it was a fantastic engraving of the last survivor of the human race cowering in the dusk beside his puny fire at the bottom of some vast, shadowy canyon—a monstrous gash into the heart of a dead world. This place was it, as near as any man would ever see it. Gordon Matthews and I camped several times on this bar in the following year, and we came to know it as the Last Man Camp.

The Lower Canyon must be about 14 miles long, and it took me two days to get through it. The place that nearly stuck me was not far above that first camp: there is an island in the river there, and an island well out into the stream usually means trouble since the current, splitting on the point of it, is thrown hard against the cliffs on either shore. The result is that each side is sheer and deep, affording no tracking beach and no poling bottom. This island was no exception to the rule; in fact, it was worse than most of these obstructions: the river raced past it in a fast riffle, and each bank was a sheer rock wall. There was only one thing to do—wade the canoe upstream from the upper point of the island until the last possible inch had been gained and the canoe floated level with the breast pockets of one's shirt. Then spring in off the river bottom, grab the paddle, and let drive with it, all out, and try to catch the tail end of a sandy beach on the right shore before being swept backwards down the riffle.

Twice I was whirled down close under the canyon wall, and the third time I made it—just. The hardest thing in making one of these crossings off an island is to balance the canoe at exactly the right angle before jumping in. An inch or two off center and the canoe will sheer as you jump—and you might as well make a fresh start. The nose of the canoe must split the current exactly, with the very slightest bias towards the shore you are making for. When you have it that way, jump and put all you know into it!

And why doesn't the canoe upset when you jump in? And what about the load? You must fetch in two or three quarts of water every time you try this stunt—surely the whole outfit must get completely soaked by the end of the day?

Well, for one thing you're not using a round-bottomed, tipply pleasure canoe: you're using a work canoe. I had a 16-foot Chestnut, Prospector Model, 36 inches wide and 14 inches deep—a canoe with beautiful lines but fairly flat-bottomed: load three or four hundred pounds of outfit into that and you've got a pretty stable canoe—something you won't upset at all easily. You can stand up and pole in it, you can crawl about over the load in it and pull yourself upstream by handholds in the canyon wall, and you can put all your weight onto the gunwale on one side of it, and still it won't upset from that cause alone.

Faille had an 18-foot freight canoe—also a Chestnut. His canoe was 46 inches wide and 18 inches deep, and when that was loaded down solid you could go for a stroll over the load and it would barely alter the trim. Faille was using a 3½ h.p. outboard, and he had it out on a homemade bracket, not off to one side as one sometimes sees them, but where it should be—directly behind the stern of the canoe. He had no use for a square-ended canoe, specially shaped to take an outboard, and, after running one down the Cache Rapid two years ago, neither have I.

As to water in the canoe, that was easily dealt with. I always laid, lengthways on the bottom, three light, dry spruce poles: over them was spread a large double-proofed tarpaulin, the "canoe tarp." One edge of this was pulled up level with the gunwale of the canoe, and the perishable part of the load—flour, sugar, ammunition, clothes, films, etc.—was then laid in the bight of this big tarp and packed solid. When this was done the ends of the tarp could be folded up, and the loose bunch of tarpaulin on the far side of the canoe could be pulled across under the thwarts and tucked in outside the section that was level with the gunwale, between it and the side of the canoe. If that was carefully done the canoe could dive through a wave in a riffle, or have six inches of rainwater slopping about in it from an overnight thunderstorm, and still the load would be perfectly dry. The three spruce poles on the floor of the canoe would allow this water to drain back into the tail whence it could be bailed. Anything like a waterproofed tent, a sleeping bag in its proofed cover, axes, cooking pots, and so forth would be packed where they were most handy, outside the tarp. A sharp, light axe always lay ready for action, under the rear seat of the canoe. The trackline of heavy sash cord lay on top of the canoe tarp, coded in such a way that it would pay out swiftly and easily, without getting snarled up, as one jumped for shore holding the line in either hand. On top of all this lay the pole, shod end to the rear, point tucked into the canoe's nose, where also was to be found a roll of birch bark for the lighting of a fire.

That passage through the Lower Canyon was the sort of thing that comes to a man perhaps once in a lifetime—if he's lucky. The scenery is the finest on the Nahanni, and the weather was perfect—clear, with cold nights and blazing hot days. And it was all strange and new: rounding a bend was like turning a page in a book of pictures; what would one see, this time, and would this next reach hold, perhaps, some insuperable obstacle? But it never did, and always one found some way around by means of some new trick with the line or the pole.

RUNNING WILBERFORCE CANYON

Bill Mason

An enthusiastic whitewater encounter in Canada's Northwest Territories

MY IDEA OF THE PERFECT river is one that has spectacular falls or canyon, or both, preferably near the end, so you've got something to look forward to, like icing on the cake. And if there's a canyon a couple of miles long and more than 200 feet deep below the falls, with rapids that might be runnable, well, that would be the river of which dreams are made.

The Hood is such a river. It flows due east through Canada's Northwest Territories for about 100 miles before swinging north and emptying into the Arctic Ocean at Bathurst Inlet. About a day's journey above the mouth, the river narrows into a red sandstone canyon, then plunges 80 feet into a churning cauldron of foam, takes a right-angle turn to the left, and plunges again, over a 100-foot drop. The two drops are Wilberforce Falls, perhaps the most spectacular in Canada. Towering spires soar from the very base of the second falls, high above the first. If you climb out along the narrow hogback ridge that provides access to one of the pinnacles, you can look down 180 feet into the depths of the canyon.

In 1985, six of us ran the Hood. Wally Schaber and I were in one canoe, Alan Whatmough and Bruce Cockburn in the second, and Gilles Couet and Gilles Levesque in the third. Because of its remoteness and its frigid water and air temperatures, the Hood is in a class by itself as a wilderness experience. It was the middle of July, and we still had to dodge ice on all the big lakes. You can imagine what that did for the water temperatures downstream. We ran the more difficult rapids with considerable apprehension.

But the whitewater we were waiting for was the canyon below Wilberforce Falls. If it were runnable, it would be beyond our wildest dreams. Below the two falls, the Hood surges through a two-mile canyon below 200-foot walls on its journey to the ocean.

We pitched camp above the falls in the pouring rain, then rushed off to have a look at the canyon. We found the scree slope that led to the base of the falls, then walked along the canyon rim, scouting rapids. They looked difficult, but we believed we could handle them, and we worked out an intricate plan of back-ferries and lines of attack. Once we got into the canyon there would be no lining or portaging and no turning back. The walls were either sheer, or steep, crumbling rock with overhangs.

As I retraced my steps along the canyon rim, I estimated the degree of difficulty and multiplied by two. Rapids always look much easier from above; waves flatten out and don't look as forbidding as they really are. I knew running those rapids deep within the canyon was going to be exciting. Schaber, Couet, and Levesque were ecstatic about the idea. Alan volunteered to photograph the run from above.

We waited out a rainy night and the next day left the canoes at the top of the scree slope, carried all the gear over the three-mile portage in the rain, and set up camp at the end of the canyon.

Even though we would be wearing wetsuits and paddling jackets, no one was very keen on attempting the canyon in cold, rainy weather. With water temperatures just above freezing, the dangers of hypothermia would have been too great. But there was also a psychological factor. The black depths of that canyon just looked too intimidating in this bleak weather.

In the morning, the sky was clear. We rushed through breakfast, put on our wetsuits, and set out for the head of the canyon, scouting the rapids again as we went. We looked for eddies. They would give us a chance to catch our breath and to bail, but there were very few. The river looked powerful, but each rapid on its own looked runnable. The holes were avoidable, the Vs clearly defined. The haystacks would give us a good ride.

We eased the boats down the scree slope. Schaber and I reached water level just as Couet and Levesque completed their front ferry to the right side of the canyon below the falls. Their skill was impressive: the water rushing downstream from the base of the falls was a seething mass of boils. The back eddy by shore raced upstream at an alarming angle. I didn't like it, and the anxiety in Wally's voice reinforced my apprehension. We would have to set an extreme angle when we exited the eddy or be drawn back toward the falls.

With the canoe facing upstream, we climbed in and began our front-ferry, but were pulled quickly toward the falls. We back-paddled furiously but went nowhere. Finally, Wally grabbed onto some rocks and dragged the canoe and me back to the eddy. On the fourth try we made it out. The boils pulled and grabbed the canoe as we ferried across the current. We were definitely not having a good time. The sheer volume and turbulence were very unsettling. We had completely underestimated the power of the water. But now that we had ferried to the far shore, there was no turning back.

We gazed up at Alan, a slim speck against the sky on the canyon rim. Levesque and Couet pushed off, ran down the side of the first rapid, and eddied out just around the bend. As we crossed the eddy line, we felt our stern sinking into a whirlpool. It was not a good feeling. This stuff was big! Bigger than anything we had ever paddled, and this was the first rapid, the one that had appeared the easiest. We should have multiplied the degree of difficulty by four or five.

By the time we pulled into the eddy with Couet and Levesque, we had lost our enthusiasm for our carefully made plans. All we wanted to do was get on with it. We paddled out of the eddy, shot by the other boat, and began to back-ferry to set up for the next rapid. It would have been a wild, exhilarating ride anywhere else, but here worry outweighed pleasure. I managed a halfhearted shout and reached under my spray skirt to get my camera out. "Forget the pictures!" Wally shouted. I looked back to protest just as the third rapid came into view. In the history of picture-taking, no camera ever went back into its box faster.

In front of us, the whole river was piling into a cliff. Schaber yelled for a back-ferry to the right. We hugged the right side of the V, which put us into the diagonal waves coming off the standing waves. We hit the diagonals broadside. The canoe rolled up on its side and without even a pause just kept going over. One instant I was upright and the next I was hanging upside down. I kicked against the bottom of the canoe, propelling myself down, and out of the spray skirt.

I struggled for the surface but there was no air, only turbulence and whitewater. My first breath was half air and half water. I was pulled under, and when I finally got another breath I caught sight of Schaber. The canoe was between us and he was swinging toward the right shore. We rode the waves of one rapid after another until I saw the blue water racing for a drop-off and a hole. I kicked away from it and lost sight of Wally as the waves engulfed me. Then I was through the worst of the rapid. Schaber was nowhere to be seen.

Suddenly, I felt the cold and the fatigue. I swung close to the right bank and pulled myself onto a ledge about a foot above water. I wondered about Schaber, Cauet, and Levesque, but could see no one. I saw no alternative, so I started to climb out of the canyon. I went as far as I could, but was stopped cold under a crumbly overhang and had to climb down. Back by the river, warm finally from exertion, I heard Schaber call from the rim above me. He had washed through a hole that had sucked his running shoes off his feet and had climbed out of the canyon in his wetsuit boots. At his direction, I swam to the other side of the river and was able to make an easier climb up the other cliff.

We headed for our camp, Wally on one side of the rim, I on the other. When our tents came into sight, I saw four figures. Everyone was accounted for, and we soon heard the full story. Couet and Levesque had seen us capsize and rushed to shore to search for us. As they peered downstream, their canoe drifted into view on the current. They had pulled it up to a ledge but a wave had lifted it free. With considerable consternation they watched it negotiate the rapid that had trashed Wally and me and then dance merrily on its way around a bend. Then they swam to the other side of the river and climbed out of the canyon. Schaber eventually spotted their canoe in an eddy below the rapids and paddled it to shore by the camp. And Couet later found the boat we had lost and was able to pry it off a rock a couple of miles downstream. The spray cover was torn, paddles gone, and Schaber's camera was missing.

There was much discussion that night about our canoeing skills. There we were with our complete spray skirt, back-ferry, high and low braces, pries and draws, pivots and backwatering, and we ended up swimming. A canoe with no spray cover and no paddlers ran everything and came through dry. It was agreed that we would have been better off just to skip the paddling and lie down in our boat.

Now when I remember the canyon below Wilberforce Falls, I am sure we have run bigger stuff with flotation in the canoe and even played in it. So why was it such a harrowing experience? Why did I try to climb out of the canyon where I was instead of swimming across immediately to the easier climb?

What made it such a nightmare was the combination of all the elements. We were many hundreds of miles from help. We could not have replaced a lost canoe. The water was icy. To enter a canyon is to go where there is no return. Having made shore, I was helpless. There was an irresistible urge to escape the canyon; we all felt it.

And then there is the old question: Why venture into a canyon like that? Why take the risk? Is it worth it? Well, there's the incredible view from the bottom of the canyon looking up as we round each bend in the river. There's the sheer thrill of running whitewater. We had wondered if we would be the first to run this stretch. The arctic shore just north of where we were is dotted with the graves of the almost 200 men who died in the attempt to be the first through the Northwest Passage. But for us being first was no big deal. We'd just wanted to run it. We didn't need a reason.

In the end, it was worth it because everything came out all right. If we had lost a canoe or if one of us had been hurt or killed, it would not have been worth it. Sooner or later someone will run it. Maybe even in a canoe, probably at lower water.

One thing Wally and I feel bad about is that we'll never know whether Couet and Levesque could have made the run. We think they could have. In any case, if you meet them on the streets of Chicoutimi (Quebec) and ask how they made out in Wilberforce Canyon, they can honestly say: "Oh, the canoe went through just fine. Hardly a drop of water in it."

READING THE RIVER

John Hildebrand

Stormbound on the Yukon River

THE WIND BLEW FROM THE southwest, from the sea, tilting the river into a billowy expanse of whitecaps. I kept the bow windward to quarter the waves so they swept past without shipping much water over the gunwales. Sometimes a large swell heaved the front of the canoe out of the water and then dropped it into the lurch with a splash. I would sooner run Five Finger Rapids in a bathtub than face the lower Yukon on a breezy day. Rainwater collected in pools in my lap and streamed down my back until my lower half was soaked. Hugging the shore, I searched for a level landing. But sheer rock cliffs ran down to the water on the right bank, and the river was too wide and wind-tossed for me to consider crossing to the leeward bank. Besides, I could barely see through the rain to the dismal far shore.

Tacking around a blind point, I landed on a pocket beach strewn with foam and driftwood. There is a great sense of relief at making landfall in rough weather, when each mile has been hard won. Quickly, I unpacked the tent and looked around for a smooth spot to erect it. Then I hesitated—fresh tracks led out of the bordering woods and made a transit of the beach. I'd seen plenty of black bear tracks before, but these were larger and more formidably spaced. Pressed into the soft yellow clay, each print was as wide across as the length of my boots and topped with five toes and radiating claw

93

points just now filling with rain. The tracks belonged to a brown bear, a coastal grizzly, and they left no less an impression on me than on the wet beach. Faced with a choice of terrors, I debated whether to take my chances with the storm-tossed river or camp here and face a sleepless night. The river was an uncertainty, but the bearish nightmare was already fully formed in my brain: a sharp snort as claws rend the tent. A great, dish-faced profile sways overhead, so near I smell the close, rancid breath. The beaded eyes are set close together; the silver fur on its humped back glistens in the moonlight. I reach for the shotgun at my side, but the mechanism jams. I open my mouth to cry out but cannot. The bear pulls me from the sleeping bag into a terrible embrace as the dream dissolves around me.

I repacked the tent and launched back into the whitecapped waves.

Landing finally in a tiny grotto formed by projecting rock spurs, I set the tent on a narrow shelf of broken shale. It looked like a place for votive candles and miraculous springs. Out of the wind and safe from night-wandering bears, I fell into a deep, dreamless sleep. For two days I remained stormbound on that ledge, protected from the storm and sealed off from the rest of the world. When I stuck my head outside the tent on the second day, I seemed to be in the middle of a cloud. The far bank was lost in fog, and the river's surface lay broken into gray waves like overlapping tiles on a slate roof.

The notes from my journal give some hint of my mood:

> August 8. Still raining. Wind from the south. I am curled in a fetal position in my sleeping bag, head tucked under the covers, listening to the rain's patter and the steady lashing of waves against the shore. Finished last of whiskey yesterday, a small thing but one of those pleasures that civilize a camping trip. Did nothing today but memorize the tent's stitchery.

I boiled water over the small kerosene stove for tea and to keep the tent warm. Wet clothes were strewn everywhere. Some were trying to dry and others I used to plug the tent's leaky corners where pools of rainwater had formed. My journal entries were becoming more cryptic and full of complaints. I had reached that dangerous point on a long journey when things break down, when the essential organization on which you depend turns to chaos. Dishes are put away dirty, clothes don't dry out, meals are simplified to a few soggy crackers and tea. Mistakes wait to happen because your mind is set not on the tasks at hand but on getting home. I started making wish lists: dry clothes, a warm bed, a drink with ice. A few books remained to read, most having been given away on the journey in small payment for some kindness. Encased in my sodden sleeping bag, knees drawn to my chest, I reread a paperback *Odyssey* with a new sympathy for the shipwrecked Odysseus—"poor fellow, kept from his friends all this while in trouble and sorrow, in that island covered with trees, and nothing but the waves all about it, in the very middle of the sea."

In the afternoon the fog lifted enough to provide clearance between the river and cloud ceiling. I bailed out my canoe and started again. The Yukon reaches its southernmost point at Roundabout Mountain, near the abandoned settlement of Ohagamiut, having looped back to nearly the latitude it started at in Whitehorse. Rounding the horn, the canoe began to pitch and yawl in heavy chop. The wind had shifted and I found myself plowing north into stinging drizzle and the teeth of a 30-knot gale. The river yawned three miles across where it swallowed an island. By ducking into side channels, I could run out of the wind until the slough rejoined the main channel and cast me back into the maelstrom. Shivering wet, my teeth chattering, I was determined now to motor on toward the next village. It was a fateful decision because soon I was too weak and thick-headed to think about putting up a tent in this wind. When my strength gave out, I would just tie up along shore and lie down in the rain for a long sleep. Each deserted bend in the river brought a new disappointment. I had nearly decided to moor the canoe to a cutbank and crawl into the alders when I saw a pair of strange lights burning ahead in the sky. They were the headlights of an airplane flying low beneath the clouds, descending upon the landing strip at Marshall.

I took a room above the store in Marshall. Few villages on the lower river have places for a visitor to stay, so it seemed great luck to find one here. The heat wouldn't come on, but I thawed out with a hot shower, my first since Tanana, and crawled exhausted between the sheets. About six o'clock I heard the downstairs door slam as the store owner left and his teenage replacement arrived. Immediately she put a love song on the record player, something current and insipid. She must have been heartsick, or maybe the record changer was broken, but she played that dreary song over and over again until the lyrics were etched in my brain. Even after she locked up for the night and went home, the words kept returning like a bad dream.

I awoke in the morning to barking dogs and the whine of two-stroke engines—the sounds of village life. Looking out a rainstreaked window, I saw a man puttering down a muddy road on his motorbike, a rifle slung across his back. Marshall sits at the base of Pilcher Mountain on a high ledge over the Yukon. Beyond the backyard clutter of woodpiles, oil cans, and clotheslines flying in the gale, the river lay puckered into whitecaps beneath a slate gray sky.

The store owner, a stocky, pleasant Eskimo named Leslie Hunter, drove me around the village in his pickup truck. Splashing down the road, Hunter pointed out the new fish-processing plant. "Lots of fish this year," he said, "but not much money." We passed a boarded-up hotel, bleached white as a whalebone, a remnant of Marshall's past as a fledgling gold camp. Two prospectors discovered gold on nearby Wilson Creek in 1913 and named the creek for the current president and the townsite for his running mate, Thomas Marshall, who had campaigned under the bromide, "What this country needs is a good five-cent cigar." The stampede to Marshall was the last major gold rush on the Yukon. Most of the village, however, seemed only a few years old. Set on barren tundra, the prefabricated housing in poster-paint colors gave Marshall the look of one of those instant Wyoming strip-mining towns. Hunter's grandfather had come from Pennsylvania to be the mining camp's first postmaster, but just as his grandson now favors the Eskimo side of the family, so had Marshall changed complexions over the years.

The truck rocked in the wind as we parked above a beach littered with tethered skiffs and miserable-looking dogs curled in the mud. I asked Leslie Hunter if any of the old miners had stayed on in Marshall. There were a few, he said. One had just died at 83, still chipping away at his claims. He'd hired a pilot to drop him at his cabin 40 miles back in the hills. When the pilot flew back a month later to check on him, he found only a burnt cabin and some charred bones in the doorway. The prospector had stockpiled Molotov cocktails for bear protection because his eyesight was too poor for aiming a rifle, and the consensus was that the gasoline bombs, not the bears, got him in the end.

Hunter told me there was another old-timer who lived just up the road, and he dropped me at Gene Tetinek's cottage. Tetinek answered the door in a plaid wool shirt and bedroom slippers, a shock of white hair falling across his forehead. Stacks of newspapers and bundled magazines lay on the floor. He sat back in an easy chair and filled his pipe from a tobacco tin. A photograph of the paddle-wheeler *Nenana* hung on the wall. We listened to the weather forecast over the Nome radio station, first in English and then in Yupik Eskimo; another storm was spiraling up the coast from the Aleutians.

When I told Tetinek of my travels, he seemed unimpressed. I had arrived too late, he said, to see the real North. Old-timers were always telling me that.

"Used to be if you wanted to settle someplace, all you had to do was throw up a log cabin, and that was that. Not anymore. The country's changed."

In the summer of 1934, Tetinek was cutting cordwood in Fort Yukon when he got the itch to travel. He paid $5 for a flimsy ratting canoe and set off down the Yukon, reaching Marshall just as gold hit $35 an ounce on the open market. He was offered a job in one of the mines, but turned it down to spend the winter outside. Hiring on as a deck hand on the steamboat *Nenana*, he retraced his route upriver, hopped a freight to the railhead at Seward, and then took a steamship to Seattle, where he hitchhiked the last leg home to Cleveland. Tetinek returned to the America of the National Recovery Act, a country of soup kitchens and bread lines. The depression was in full swing, so he never even bothered looking for work. The next summer he returned to Marshall to operate a hydraulic hose in the Willow Creek mine. The hose shot stream water from the nozzle with enough ballistic force to strip the soil down to gold-bearing bedrock. When the gold mines shut down after the war, he operated a trading post until retiring.

I asked him why, with the price of gold so high, the large mines hadn't started up again.

"It isn't the price of gold, it's the price of everything else. Especially freight, if something breaks down and you need to have it shipped up. Last year I ordered a boat from Seattle, and the freight cost more than the boat!"

Once a year Tetinek flew to Anchorage for a change of pace, but when I asked why he didn't move there permanently, it was clear he'd soured on the city.

"What would I do there? You need a car to get anywhere. If you have a snow tractor, you need a permit."

One thing bothered me about Tetinek's story. I had seen a ratting canoe in a museum in Fort Yukon. Built of canvas stretched over a spruce frame, they are employed in the spring for hunting muskrat and look as tippy as a pea pod.

"Where did you stow your supplies?"

"Supplies?" The tone of his voice implied my own needs were extravagant. "Plenty of room for a sleeping bag, a rifle, some grub. What more could you possibly need?"

Before I checked out of my room above the store, Leslie Hunter warned me of three bad spots between Marshall and St. Marys, "stretches where the wind blows one way and the river goes the other." He had no map and so depended upon his words and the urgency of his gestures to convey the downriver landmarks, the islands and bends that I was to watch for. But I didn't pay much attention: I was in too big a hurry to leave during what appeared to be a lull in the storm. Immediately after leaving Marshall, I crossed a half mile of open water to a long island that broke the wind blowing off the main channel. I had completely forgotten about the first of the bad spots until, rounding the lee of the island, I stumbled into it. The wind was blowing a terrific gale. The waves broke with a sigh, lifting the canoe so that it teetered on the crest of a wave before plunging into the sea green trough. The major problem of small-boat navigation in heavy swells is keeping boat and waves on a parallel course. I would quarter the smaller waves, then align the bow to meet the oncoming rollers. Five inches of freeboard were all that separated me from the river. Yet as long as the waves didn't come from the side, breaking over the gunwales, the canoe would ride out the chop. Each roller rushing headlong toward the canoe seemed fated to swamp it, but each time the crest fell short, the little boat riding over the wave instead of beneath it.

The Yukon's course became more erratic, describing corkscrews and oxbow turns, as it cut away at the headlands. Changing direction, the river moved in and out of the wind, and for long stretches at a time I had smooth sailing. The second bad spot was Dogtooth Bend, a several-mile loop around a cuspid of tundra. At the bend, the channel I was following intersected with an even larger channel, and the waves, instead of charging at the bow, suddenly swept down from the stern. The canoe surfed forward on the crest of a wave heading for shore. Unable to change course for fear of presenting the boat sideways to the swells, I watched helplessly as the backs of green rollers rushed past to break in a line on the beach. Between waves, the prop scraped sand and kicked out of the water with an awful whine. Then the outboard stalled. The canoe lurched sideways and began to ship water. With no power or steerage, there was nothing I could do but tilt the engine up and paddle to keep the bow straight as the waves deposited me ashore.

The far end of the beach was not pounded nearly so hard by the surf. Lining the canoe to the sheltered end, I cast off again. The rain had stopped, and a sickly yellow light shone below the clouds. I turned into a leeward slough where the alder banks drew close, and the wind's tumult died as suddenly as if a window had been shut. A red fox trotted along the shore, tail unfurled like a pennant. For miles I followed this interior passage before stopping on a damp sandbar for the evening.

The edge of the sandbar was muddy, and as I carried gear ashore from the canoe my rubber boots pulled from the mire with a sucking noise. I shared the sandbar with an enormous spruce log propped up on its roots and pointing downriver. Scoured from a riverbank by spring ice, its branches sheared off to nubs, the great log had rafted downstream in floodwater to be stranded here, smooth and polished. Its trunk sheltered my tent from the wind and its roots made resinous kindling for my fire.

Walking down to the river to wash my dinner dishes, I found that I wasn't alone. Voices and soft laughter carried faintly from a fish camp at the end of the slough, and somehow this discovery made me feel more forlorn. When you travel alone, it's not the strangeness of places that tugs at your heart but the way things are the same. The voices spoke in Yupik, but I could make out the peculiar cadences of family talk, the small jokes and affections. The few risky moments I'd recently had on the river only sharpened my sense of isolation. One of the most human of fears, I think, must be of dying alone. After a close call, we want someone to share our relief; we want to matter, not in any general way, but to someone in particular. I was tired of being a floater. When I could see past the bitterness of my failed marriage, I had to admit that, in balance, the good memories outweighed the bad. And, since memories were all I had at the moment, I wanted to cherish them. Crawling into the tent, I began a long-postponed letter to my ex-wife. I meant to finally clear the air between us, so it was really a goodbye letter, but since we hadn't spoken civilly in two years it was a hello, as well.

The sky cleared the next morning. The sun felt warm against my back as I loaded the canoe and headed down the slough toward the main channel. Nobody was home at the fish camp except for a husky pup tethered to a stake.

The Yukon spread out windless and benign, a deeper shade of blue than the sky. Fishing boats bobbed in the distance—the truest measure of good weather. The rough water and bad weather behind me, I felt expansive, no longer in a hurry. The end of the trip seemed in sight. With the proper attitude, I thought, one could make a bargain with the river, stay on its good side.

I trolled up to a shovel-nosed skiff. An Eskimo fisherman and his son, perhaps the voices I'd heard the night before, were untangling a burbot from their net. The burbot had the head of a toad and body of an eel and glared malignantly from the bottom of the boat as it expired.

How far, I asked, to Pilot Station.

"You're almost there. You'll see it right around the next bend."

The Yukon formed a T as it bent sharply to the southwest and the Chuilnak River entered from the east. Racing around the bend, I saw the blue-roofed houses of Pilot Station in a saddle between two hills. The village could not have been more than a mile away, so I steered a direct course for it, cutting diagonally across the river.

Then everything went wrong.

A blast of wind caught me as I cleared the bend. Funneled down the narrow flume of the channel, the wind curled the river back on itself. Billowy waves loomed ahead like a range of green hills dusted with snow. Too late, I remembered Leslie Hunter's warning about the final bad stretch of river. It was here.

If I headed straight for shore, the waves would smash the canoe broadside and capsize it, so I had no choice but to steer straight into the green wall of water. The first swell lifted the bow into the air, the horizon tilted, and the canoe slid down the long valley of the wave. Climbing the next crest, I tried to count the oncoming rollers, wondering how they would break, trying to read the one that would finally crash over the bow and swamp the boat.

The sensation was of being propelled forward by a mob, a noise roaring in my ears, unable to stop or turn but only keep pace and stay alert. The shore lay a quarter-mile swim in either direction, but it might as well have been half an ocean away. If I capsized, silt would fill my pockets and boots and I would do the Australian crawl in slow motion to the bottom.

Seagulls careened overhead. Safe on two counts, the gulls pivoted their small white heads to see if I had any fish in the boat or if perhaps I was a fish. At first I felt a perverse thrill as the canoe smacked into a wave and still emerged upright. But knowing that I was almost certainly going to drown soon filled me with rage. At the fisherman for not warning me. At the river for letting me come this far only to drown in plain sight of blue-roofed houses. But mostly at myself for being so careless, so stupid as to ruin a perfectly good life by throwing it away. Shouting into the wind, I prayed the most basic prayer: Save me. Spare my life.

A roller swept the canoe up, then slammed it down into the hollow so hard that the gas tank nearly jumped into my lap. Between one terrible crest and the onslaught of another, I began veering ever so slightly toward the right bank, then straightening the bow before the next roller hit. Slowly, I edged farther from the foamy peaks until the canoe slipped into the sidewash. Then suddenly I was out of it, in calm water, the village shining ahead.

"I saw you in trouble out there," a young fisherman said as I hauled the canoe out of the river. He was bailing the bilge water from his skiff with a plastic pail. "But there was nothing I could do. You have to cross directly in front of the village to avoid those big waves. Lots of people drown where you crossed. It's a real bad spot."

On wobbly legs, I walked up the beach past the Russian church and up a hill to the little post office to mail the letter I'd written the night before. The mail plane had just arrived, and I had to wait in line while the mail was sorted. But it was a pleasant wait. People joked about the delay and enjoyed the sunshine. Standing there, among strangers, I found myself smiling, too, and thought: How amazing all of this is—simply being alive! I was elated because my life had been handed back to me when it seemed almost certainly lost. I felt the wind in my hair and noticed that my red baseball cap was gone, the one drunken Lonnie had given me long ago in Circle. It must have blown off in midriver and was now drifting to rest somewhere in the delta.

SUMMER NORTH OF SIXTY

James Raffan

A canoeing foray above the Arctic Circle

THE END IS CLOSING QUICKLY. Settling into the rhythm of the day's paddling, we all scan the hills opposite for sight of last evening's wolves. Nothing. But I am silently warmed by the thought that somewhere on those steep, greened slopes are at least three pairs of eyes, probably four, watching us leave their territory.

Quickly, however, there is no energy or time for shore-watching. The river since the mouth of the Mara is squeezed between ever-closing banks that rise 600 and 700 feet off the water. In the canoes we're left feeling small, insignificant, and caught on a predetermined course leading—whether we like it or not—to the sea. But, instead of being fearful of the bigness of the land and of the seeming inevitability of our future with the river, riding with the water as it drops between ten and twenty feet every mile is a focused and very satisfying experience.

There are no falls or major rapids marked on this stretch on the map, but with the dramatic change in elevation, we're wary, although not quite wary enough. Inside corners are usually the safe place to be, because there is always a back eddy to pull into, providing time to bail should the going get rough. But, on this occasion, in a series of switchbacks in the river, staying to the left side of the river turns one inside corner into the outside of a much-more-tumultuous bend. It is all Gail and I can do—no time for elegant ferrying—to dig deep and drive the canoe diagonally across the river to a rip current on the inside. The lateness of the maneuver sweeps us sideways through standing waves at the brink of this corner drop. We ignore the water that splashes into the boat as a result of our speed, thinking only of getting away from the eight-foot waves and swirling currents on the outside of the corner that will surely swamp us. The river drops away to our left, giving the impression of paddling down a set of steep garden stairs: for a moment I feel as if my canoe seat is a stool, and I'm perched high above the water. Adrenalin-charged strokes see us to the inside of the bend, and amid flying ribbons of spray mixed with celebratory hoots of high adventure, we pull into the inside eddy to bail.

"Phew! That was close," Gail says, twisting in her seat to have a look at the amount of water that has collected in the heavy end of the boat. Radiant life in her sun-weathered complexion shines through lingering spray that rolls off her face and onto her life-jacket. "We're getting cocky, but I love it!"

Two or three eddys later on this river roller coaster, we pull in for another bailing session and find a foam-covered hand-carved spruce canoe yoke, mute reminder of someone else's experience with this wild section of the Burnside. I think of the politician and his "polar jet" crew and wonder if this was their upset, and if it was ever reported via radio to the Yellowknife control tower and thus to the folks back home. Our good fortune on the bad corner, we realize, did have a large element of luck. The yoke is enough to renew our commitment to scouting rapids before shooting them, even if there are no marked sets in this stretch of river.

We lunch on the Arctic Circle, the earthly line above which the sun is visible for 24 hours, for at least one day, during the summer months. The occasion links us to the geometry of the solar system and allows us to celebrate the 23.5-degree tilt of the earth's axis, relative to the line joining the center of the earth with the center of the sun, that gives our planet the seasons. Ninety degrees minus the tilt of the earth gives the latitude of the Arctic Circle. Without the tilt there would be no seasons; day and night would be 12 hours each everywhere on the planet. More importantly, there would be no Arctic Circle on which to build our northern fantasy.

For some people, the edge of the forest is the place where north begins, and rightly so, because this is a line, or at least a zone, that can be seen. For others, north begins with the line of continuous permafrost. But for us the Arctic Circle, the invisible line of latitude marking 66.6 degrees above the equator, is more significant than either of those. The Arctic Circle may be geometrically derived and have a rational explanation, but for us the mythology of the Circle—the Circle's magic that has found its way into northern songs and stories—is of great significance. Crossing the Arctic Circle places us firmly, if only in our imaginations, in the true north of this vast country. Paddling across the Arctic Circle is probably one of the most Canadian, if not romantic, acts of our lives. Why not use it as an excuse to drain the dregs of whiskey from the last of our Sigg bottles and sing a rousing chorus of "This Land Is Your Land"?

Sometime later a young golden eagle makes its way into view, flying up the valley. As if it just crossed an invisible borderline marking the territory of another bird of prey, two peregrine falcons dive out of the sun and strike the surprised eagle. They wheel, climb, and swoop again, this time turning the bottom of their U-drive and striking the belly of the eagle on their way back up. The big eagle tries to dodge the striking falcons, but to no avail: it's like a sausage-sized cecropia-moth caterpillar attempting to evade a couple of angry hornets.

The speed with which the falcons drop from the sky is difficult to comprehend. They are supposed to be one of the fastest birds around, credited with reaching 100 miles per hour on occasion. From our vantage point, the remembered statistics mean very little. The fiesty little falcons beat their wings to a point high above the eagle and then tuck them in, leaving only little missile vanes protruding. They seem to drop faster than free-falling stones. The eagle, the majestic eagle, is no match in the categories of speed and agility, but it perseveres, and as it passes overhead and further upstream, the falcons desist and disappear into the craggy green hills. Crossing the falcon's territorial boundary is a lesson that has cost the young eagle a flight feather on its right wing, but the encounter with the falcons has, presumably, been a lesson of value.

The Arctic Circle, the aerial show, the river, the hills, the rapids—all of these sights and events are laid down in sequence in my imagination, creating a special kind of bond to the corridor through which we are travelling. Knowing that eagles live here, that falcons live here, and that they have trouble getting along from time to time, is all part of an increasingly complex set of understandings I have about this land through which we're travelling. Where we are at this moment has a number on the Universal Transmercator Grid; it has a citation relative to the Arctic Circle and the ordered reticule of meridian and parallel lines of which it is a part. Where we are on the Burnside River has a time and distance from our end-point at Bathurst Inlet. But, in the fullness of this experience of journeying through the Burnside River valley, all of those place-holders seem foreign and somehow insignificant. Where are we right now? We are in the overlap of that golden eagle and those two angry falcons. We are paddling between terraced green hills. We are downstream from a tricky switchback in the river. We are on a long, sloping water corridor that is dropping to ocean tidewater at a rate of 15 feet per mile. We are at a high point in our lives. We are here.

IV

GRAND CANYON

BROKEN WATERS SING

Gaylord Staveley

Rowing a dory into the cataracts of Grand Canyon

HANCE IS THE WIDEST RAPID. Red Canyon comes tributary there on the left and its boulders have been flood-thrust out into a river that is 75 yards wide or more. Some of its boulders had not been carried far when the river current seized them and pushed them downstream and they became a cobbled left-bank promontory that narrows the rapid harshly, farther down. But many other boulders have been driven nearly across the 75 yards, or half of it, or a third of it, and bedded themselves, and refused to be dislodged by the river, even the old, strong river. They lie there, some big, some huge, all through it, tearing long shreds of froth down the water, offering ragged boat chutes between, then blocking them with boulders, and the Colorado runs hard and drops a fast 30 feet through it all. Hance is rated nine or ten on the one-to-ten scale of difficulty.

We always study the rapid hoping there is a way through, yet knowing, really, we'll have to line it because we've had to ever since the dam. There used to be a way through Hance for rowboats at certain levels of runoff, working a completely lightened boat down along the left through the rocks and holes, passing near the promontory that narrows the rapid, and landing just below it. But it was done on natural river, on a volume that doesn't come any more. And a few rocks seem to have changed position.

Once again we took the time to look for that old route. Then, not seeing it, or one that would materialize with the lowering water that was on its way, we turned our attention to the lining route.

In lining, the handling of the bow line is very critical. There are usually sections of a lining course down which a boat can be allowed to slide at the current's speed, restrained only by men controlling the strong, hundred-foot line. A boat at the end of its line, pulled by fast water, behaves very much like a kite—a 600-pound one. You can "fly" it in the current and let it down through the rocks where you want it to go only if you're standing in the right place with the other end of the line, just as you can work a flying kite through a grove of trees only by walking the right ground. Fred or Don or I nearly always handle the bow line, with someone one or two steps behind to coil and recoil as it is let out and taken up. The line must always be ready to loop out smoothly as mono-filament from a spinning reel; it is zipping out through our hands several yards a second and we are braced against the boat in the current. If a coil snarls behind our hands, we can be jerked out into the river—or let the river have the boat; a choice that is not at all clear-cut, for there are times when one must make surprising choices to maximize or minimize, or make possible or make probable. A dependable coiler is insurance against having to make such choices.

Don and Fred and I became the cadre for the first letdown, with Doug, Dan, Chuck, and Walt wading into the water or crawling out over the rocks, to help the Norm past the difficult places. Don and I took the bow line, he coiling, and Fred boarded the stern deck to be with the boat when it grounded. We soaked the coil so the line wouldn't burn our hands going out and Doug and Chuck, life-jacketed as were we all, walked the boat out into chest-deep river bottomed with rounded, slippery boulders. "Ready?" called Doug.

"Ready out here," answered Fred.

"Ready, Don?" I asked over my shoulder.

"Ready."

They pushed the *Norm* out a few feet more and the current began to purchase it, gradually at first, then more strongly, drawing it down toward a cluster of rocks. We were on hand signals now because of the roar of a hundred holes out in Hance and the distance between us. I squeezed the line a little more, increasing its drag through my fingers, feeling it instantly warmer in spite of its wetness; the boat slowed a little; Fred's arms went straight up; we braced and held. The boat stopped just above a mid-chute rock. He dropped his arms, then circled an index finger over his head slowly and we eased him down until the boat stopped against a rock.

Fred got out on it, pushed the boat past, and got back on the stern. We let him down a few more yards; sitting with his legs over the transom he kicked away from one rock, then another, then another. Within a few dozen yards we had let the *Norm* down into a pool that was fed by a fast chute, and drained by another that left it laterally toward the rapid. We grounded the boat there on submerged rocks with Fred holding it in place; then Don and I moved down the shallows along shore, he recoiling the line as we went. We worked our way out above the fast pool onto rocks that gave us our angle of control. Ready again, checking everyone, we held the boat, its pointed bow parting the thrusting current as Fred set it away from the rock, not going with it this time. I played the boat in the current until it seemed properly positioned, then let it run and, as the stern flanked the lateral chute, whipped the bow line; the boat swung and the side current caught it and took it into the chute, and down around the corner, and grounded it on a large flat rock, barely covered.

Fred and several others tugged and skidded it over into the head of a pool below, standing in swift water on dangerously slippery rocks. While that was being done, Don and I repositioned and recoiled the line, taking a station on big rocks overlooking the boat, as close as we could for maximum letdown length in the next step of the operation. Now the boat would have to run the length of a long, fast pool, be "flown" directly into the head of a crooked chute going back out into deep river, then when it washed through that, be pulled into the lee of rocks just below. Having gotten it off the large flat rock and into the head of the pool, we let the current have it, but it was pushed down and against the shore side of the pool several times before we found the right water, and each time had to be dragged back up against the strong current and swung out again. Finally it caught the proper zone of the fast water and, as it came opposite the chute, a whip of the line spun to the stern of the chute and the leaving water caught it and swept it through into calmness below, with only a few feet of bow line remaining in our coil. The boat was now just above a bouldered promontory, in the lee of eight-foot rocks. There was no current to play it in, and we could only hold it there until one of the men climbed out through fast chutes and rocks to bring it in against the left bank. There the oars were replaced and a run of a few dozen yards made along the shore as closely as possible, down to the lower "beach," which was actually a coarsely bouldered shore. The river, reacting to its confinement by the promontory, surged badly there and it was necessary to haul the *Norm* and each succeeding boat onto the rocks above the lifting-dashing action of the waves for the reloading.

Lining the *Norm* took 45 minutes. We made one or two small changes in the lining course and the next boat took 40. As we became practiced, and the others worked into the team, we reduced the time to 25 minutes per boat. Meanwhile our passengers had carried not only their own gear but that of their boatman down to the lower beach, over difficult boulders and a high, hot, sandy bench. We finished the last boat just as receding water was beginning to make the smoothly working procedure more difficult, about noon, and made lunch before starting into the Upper Granite Gorge.

The strata come up sharply in the vicinity of Hance, and the gorge begins where the tailwaves are still dissipating. The first mile contains some rather lyric geology and I thought I might work out something to ease Mary's mind, but all I could contrive was:

> *Shinumo Quartzite.*
> *Hakatai Shale;*
> *A mile to the Granite,*
> *Get ready to bail.*

and I decided to keep it to myself. In a mile the Vishnu had pitched up to become the somber foundation of the other layers—hard, shiny black, imposing crooked narrowness on the river and the boats. Little grows on it. There is no soil, no flatness. No room even for scraps of shore. Black cliffs right to the water. The Granite Gorge felt again, and always will, like an ancient place, a Genesis place.

Twenty minutes after leaving Hance, we made the sharp turn of gorge to the right that is the advance landmark for Sockdologer, and then could hear its voice. "Sock" has one of the louder voices in the Grand Canyon; it is one of the larger and longer rapids. Powell named it: sockdologer, a corruption of the word "doxology," was a popular slang term of his day for something unusually large or decisive. But even if one's vocabulary didn't advise a stop to reconnoiter, one's ears would.

Staying well to the left side of the river to avoid the thrust of the main current, we nosed the boats into quiet water in the lee of projecting slabs, and tied. The shoulder of the gorge was steep and the dark, indurated rock full of midday sun and too hot to press against; we could even feel it through our shoes. Hand-and-footing our way up to a vantage point was impossible; we had to keep our feet under us and scale the wall with no more than a quick push at the hot rock when a foot slipped or we lost balance. Dislodged slabs and hunks hitting the bedrock below clanged as if they were falling on iron. When we had gone 50 feet up, and a few rods downstream, we could see Sock spread out below us.

"Hasn't changed any," said Fred. "Still big as hell." It was. There was the big tongue, pouring down in midriver into a backbone of immense wavestacks that ran for 300 yards before washing out in the quieter water; left of the stacks, river badly torn and thrashed by ledges and boulders; on the right, the wall pushing in its great breakerlike rolls of water much higher than a boatlength from trough to crest. Right of center, between the backbone of waves and the breakerlike rolls, we could point out an aisle of lesser waves. That aisle is where we usually run Sock, and it seems running through there as if the whole rapid is above you.

The water was moving off the tongue to the right so that it swerved into the right-side rollers. To avoid them we'd have to stay left on the tongue, a tactic that was complicated by a deep lateral hole coming out from the upper left—a hole we could not see into but could infer from the plunge of water over a sharp brink and a trail of froth angling out just below. We studied the course a long time so everyone would feel it was critical, watching occasional pieces of wood from a flash flood somewhere float down the tongue at different places, saying "a little farther right than that one," or "about a boatwidth left of where that one went," until everyone had his own visual measurement made. Then there came a moment that could be felt, when the talk all but stopped and the fidgeting increased, a time when everyone was ready and if we waited much longer they wouldn't be. We eased ourselves back down over the burning, clanging rock hunks, stopping partway down to see the head of the rapid more nearly as it would look from the boats. When we had returned to them the hole and the froth were completely out of sight below the brink.

For the first hundred feet we stayed left of midriver, unable to see anything beyond the smooth horizon of water where Sock started its long rampaging 25-foot drop. The roar was awesome and the tawny water pulled us toward it between the black walls. The last tailwaves started coming into view, and then in a few seconds most of the rapid, slanting down and away, a field of wild water not showing much of the pattern of stacks and rollers that had been so obvious from high on the rocks. The mound of water just above the hole then appeared, and beyond it the line of foam trailing obliquely out onto the lower tongue. The separate sound of the hole surged into focus and we moved slightly left to take just a little more of the mound above it—then we were over the mound and through the foam and down the tongue and into the waves and had found the long safe aisle and everything in the rapid seemed to be rising above us as high as the gorge walls themselves and about to crash down and fill us but none of it did, and we bobbed out below, wet, but with only three or four inches of water aboard. Looking back, I could only keep track of the other boats by their different distances from the *Norm*, and none was in sight except when it rose on a crest. The lower part of Sock has historically been a troublemaker, and only when all boats were beyond the tailwaves did it seem safe to relax.

The hot sun nearly dried us before we had drifted two more miles to Grapevine Rapid. "Grape" drops only 16 feet, but is wetter and longer than Sock. To study it we again had to climb the blistering black schist, from where we could look down on a tongue that was truncated by a row of holes just above the beginning of the tailwaves, and right and left sides that were torn into turbulence by jagged, close-set walls. The foot of the rapid ran partly into, partly past, a black buttress of the left wall, and beyond that the tailwaves ran on, out of sight around a corner. Grape is easily a half-mile long.

Standing above Grapevine we began reviewing the run of Sock, our first chance to do so. Some of the men said they had recognized a number of the waves as they passed them, which was encouraging; some of them said they couldn't tell very well where they were in the rapid. But our Sock run had been one of our best. Looking back for them as they came through, I had seen that each was where he should have been, and it was dramatic to watch them come, each in turn, through the last of the tailwaves. If we could get seven-for-seven through Grape we should have no more problem rapids that day; Bright Angel Creek was just six miles farther.

We decided to slip off the tip of the tongue to the right, taking on a wet lateral wave to miss the truncating holes, then to quarter slightly left and pull for the middle. There was a zone of relatively smooth water between the tongue and beginning of the tailwaves in which we calculated we could get three strong quartering strokes before having to turn the stern back into the turbulence. After that we could only ride it out, a wave at a time.

I didn't see them again, except the *Camscott* right behind me, until we were a mile farther down the river. The buttressing schists cut off the view and the tailwaves seemed to go on forever, but when they had finally subsided we found an eddy and waited. One by one, six boats came around the corner, bailing as we had done. When Doug came into sight in the "tail" position we moved out and caught the current again.

RIVER RUNNERS
OF THE GRAND CANYON

David Lavender

Reading the texture of the chasm

THE RIVER IS PLACID HERE, but for several minutes the roar of water ahead of the neoprene rafts has been growing louder, pulsing between the cliffs. Then suddenly the flat surface drops out of sight, its place taken by coils of spray tossed upward by whatever lies below.

The boatmen pull ashore, tie up, and with the passengers following worm through the tamarisk and scramble across a hillside littered with boulders to the head of the falls. A big one, rated up toward eight on the scale of difficulty river runners have developed over the years to evaluate rough water. The guides study it carefully, looking for whatever changes may have occurred since last they traversed it—changes caused either by shifts in the position of hazardous boulders or, more generally, by differences in the volume of water.

Back in the boats, each oarsman rows into the middle of the current. As he nears the brink, he lets his craft drift sideways while he stands for a last look at what lies ahead. Almost invariably the accelerating water gathers into a broad, smooth V, or tongue, that licks hungrily down into the masses of churned water below. There is no turning back now, but there are opportunities for last-second adjustments. By pivoting quickly with his oars, the boatman can shift his course enough to gain the exact spot he had selected earlier, from the bank, as the best one for entering the maelstrom. Once in the turmoil he guides himself by checking on markers—bushes, distinctive rocks, or even transverse waves in the rapid—that he memorized during his study.

The run takes less than a minute. On rare occasions a boat flips—turns over—but nearly always the passengers, buoyed by their life jackets, are able to hang onto it and ride through unscathed. Far more often the boat reaches the bottom of the rapid still upright, the passengers still aboard. Some of the rafts shipped only a few cupfuls of water during the run, while others in the same group filled to the brim. Whatever the case, the passengers are exhilarated. They have had an adventure, but, curiously, most of them know very little about why the rapids that provide the adventure happen to be where they are.

One facile explanation has it that rough water occurs when boulders fall from the canyon walls into a swift current. Certainly masses of rock now and then do slump off the cliffs; the light-colored spots on some precipices are clear remnants of such happenings. In Cataract Canyon, just below the junction of the Green and Colorado rivers, boulder falls have indeed caused rapids. Seldom in the Grand Canyon, however. With few exceptions (the giant boulders in Boulder Narrows and Harding rapids, for example) the tumbling rocks seldom have enough momentum to roll across the talus slopes at the foot of the cliffs into the river. When they do reach the water, they generally cause nothing more than a little fretting.

Riverside walls composed of very hard rock, as in the Upper Granite Gorge of the Grand Canyon, hold the river to a narrow span and with their jaggedness create turbulence. "Ledges of rock jut into the stream," John Wesley Powell noted during his pioneering run through the gorge in 1869, "their tops sometimes just below the surface, sometimes rising a few or many feet above; the island ledges and island pinnacles and island towers break the swift course of the stream into chutes and eddies and whirlpools." And then he adds almost casually, "We soon reach a place where a creek comes in from the left, and, just below, the channel is choked with boulders, which have washed down this lateral channel and formed a dam, over which there is a fall . . . "

Right there is the key. Most rapids in the Grand Canyon are formed by tremendous outwashes of boulders from side streams. These deltas, or boulder fans as they are sometimes called, often reach entirely across the channel and extend downstream, in the water and on the banks, for a quarter-mile or more. They are very beautiful, for they are made up of masses of water-polished stone of many colors and sizes that have been hewn from thousands of feet of strata of different composition—souvenirs of hundreds of millions of years of geologic history.

There is a paradox here. Some of the boulders in the mass are as big as small houses, and the river is unable to move them out of the way, rage at them though it will. Yet they have been brought down through lateral channels that are either dry during normal times or, at the most, contain only small creeks. How can this be?

Powell's explanation on entering Marble Gorge contains a hint, though not a very clear one. "We have learned to observe closely the texture of the rock. In softer strata we have a quiet river, in harder we find rapids and falls. Below us are the limestones and hard sandstones which we found in Cataract Canyon. This bodes toil and danger." To put the matter another way, soft strata erode easily into small fragments that gradually wash away as sediment. The canyon broadens; side streams flow more gently. Hard stone, on the other hand, forms cliffs. Drainage channels from the rim are narrow and steep. When occasional cloudbursts pour down them, the water attains awesome power. George Simmons and David Gaskill of the United States Geological Survey have translated the abstraction into mathematics. "If the speed of a body of water is doubled then its ability to transport is increased by 2 cubed, or 8 times; if the speed is trebled, the transporting power is increased by a factor of 27."

Consider the experience Robert Brewster Stanton and a small party of surveyors encountered in 1889 while climbing a side gulch out of Marble Canyon during a heavy summer rain:

> It seemed to us as if the whole edge of the canyon [i.e., of the side gulch] had begun to move. Little streams rapidly growing into torrents came over the hard top stratum from every crevice and fell on the softer slope below. In a moment they changed into streams of mud . . . undermining huge loose blocks of the harder strata. . . . As the larger blocks plunged ahead of the stream, they crashed against other blocks lodged on the slopes, and, bursting with an explosion like dynamite, broke into pieces, while the fragments flew into the air, and as the whole conglomerate mass of water, mud, and flying rocks came down the slopes to where we were, it looked as if nothing could prevent us from being buried.

Such avalanches lodge in the bottom of the side gully and, if the storm continues, are swept on into the river. There they back the water up into still pools, some a mile long. Soon, of course, the river finds ways through the blockade. The currents converge on the openings, creating the V-shaped tongues described earlier, and then plunge on into the looser masses of boulders that make up the lower part of the delta.

Any jagged rock in fast water is a threat. Still worse is a giant-sized "hole" created when part of the river rushes across the top of a huge boulder and drops down its backside like a waterfall. The plunge blasts a pit into other swirls that have been sweeping around the lower parts of the boulder. The resulting compression forces the water up into a vast standing wave, sometimes 15 feet high, on the down side of the hole. Its crest, exploding at intervals into bursts of spray, often curls back upstream, to drop thunderously into the vortex it borders.

Motor-driven, flexible rafts that drive fast and straight into the hole and the standing wave beyond it can generally break through the barrier, though the raft may be folded back almost into a right angle during the process. Wooden boats—material all early runners used—are less supple. If one of them hits at the crest of a standing wave at an angle, topples back, turns sideways perhaps, and is churned around and around until finally the current spits it out—well, it is better to have figured out in advance a course that will enable one to avoid the hole without cracking up on the boulders that flank it.

Sometimes the deltas that create rapids also squeeze the current against the cliff on the opposite side of the river. The cliff's unyielding faces and projecting snouts drive powerful reflex waves back into the channel, often at angles that can catch a boat sideways and roll it over in a twinkling. Nor is internal wildness the only problem. Often strong eddies flow backwards between the central storm of rough water and the shore. The "shear line" dividing the eddy from the downward flowing currents can be abrupt and powerful; an oar-powered raft caught inside the eddy often has trouble breaking out. Then there is downstream turbulence, particularly noticeable at times of high water. The accelerating currents in the rapid, both those on the surface and deep down, intermingle at different velocities. Air captured in the rapid by spray increases the turmoil. The churning gathers into clots beneath the surface and often will travel hundreds of yards before breaking upward in whirlpools strong enough to spin a boat completely around and sometimes even tip one over. At other times huge "boils" erupt like bubbles in a kettle of thick, heated soup.

There are about 150 rapids in the Grand Canyon above the farthest extensions of Lake Mead. (The count varies somewhat with the level of the river.) Their total length is roughly 25 miles, or nine percent of the canyon's length. In those 25 miles the river drops 1,100 feet, or approximately half of the total descent from Lees Ferry at the head of the canyon to the Grand Wash Cliffs at its foot. So the Colorado is by no means all foam and thunder. There are marvelous stretches of silence, where the iridescent water, gleaming with braids of light and shadow, glides like rippling silk. In places, the walls rise directly from the water, their bases beautifully sculptured and polished by tens of thousands of years of silt-laden currents. In other places, where the strata are soft, the cliffs draw back from the river, revealing tier upon tier of creased and colored rock, one of the greatest geologic storybooks on earth.

This overwhelming majesty is generally what one remembers after the excitement of the running of the rapids has faded. Still, boatmen and boatwomen, following the beat of many drums, have spent more than a century learning first how to ride the complex torrent and then developing the equipment needed to bring the adventure within reach of thousands of outdoor enthusiasts each year. Their triumphs and mishaps, their connivings, comedies, and tragedies are the burden of the pages that follow.

It is an American epic. Fittingly, two legendary heroes, one Indian and one white, set its tone and, in the fashion of all enduring myths, give meaning to its otherwise haphazard events.

THE ROMANCE
OF THE COLORADO RIVER

Frederick S. Dellenbaugh

An account of the historic journey down the Colorado with Major John Wesley Powell

IT WAS NOW THE BEGINNING of September, but the water and the air were not so cold as they had been the year before in Cataract Canyon, and we did not suffer from being so constantly saturated. Running on the next day following the Bright Angel camp, we found the usual number of large rapids, in one of which a wave struck the steering oar and knocked Jones out of the boat all but his knees, by which he clung to the gunwale, nearly capsizing us. We found it impossible to help him, but somehow he got in again.

The river was everywhere very swift and turbulent. One stretch of three and a half miles we ran in 15 minutes. There were numerous whirlpools, but nothing to stop our triumphant progress. On the 2nd of September there were two portages, and twenty rapids run, in the fifteen miles made during the day. Many of these rapids were very heavy descents. That night we camped above a bad-looking place, but it was decided to run it in the morning. Three-quarters of a mile below camp there was a general disappearance of the waters. We could see nothing of the great rapid from the level of the boats, though we caught an occasional glimpse of the leaping, tossing edges, or tops, of the huge billows rolling out beyond into the farther depths of the chasm.

About eight o'clock in the morning all was ready for the start. The inflated life preservers, as was customary in our boat, were laid behind the seats where we could easily reach them. The Major put his on, a most fortunate thing for him as it turned out, but we who were at the oars did not for the reason before mentioned, that they interfered with the free handling of the boat. The men of the *Canonita* took positions where they could observe and profit by our movements. Then out into the current we pushed and were immediately swept downward with ever-increasing speed toward the center of the disturbance, the black walls springing up on each side of the impetuous waters like mighty buttresses for the lovely blue vault of the September sky, so serenely quiet. Accelerated by the rush of a small intervening rapids our velocity appeared to multiply till we were flying along like a railway train.

The whole width of the river dropped away before us, falling some 25 or 30 feet, at least, in a short space. We now saw that the rapid was of a particularly difficult nature, and the order was given to attempt a landing on some rocks at its head, on the left. At the same instant this was seen to be impossible. Our only safety lay in taking the plunge in the main channel.

We backwatered on our oars to check our speed a trifle, and the next moment with a wild leap we went over, charging into the roaring, seething, beating waves below. Wave after wave broke over us in quick succession, keeping our standing-rooms full. The boat plunged like a bucking bronco, at the same time rolling with fierce violence. As rapidly as possible we bailed with our kettles, but the effort was useless. At length, as we neared the end, an immense billow broke upon our port bow with a resounding crack.

The little craft succumbed. With a quick careen she turned upside down, and we were in the foaming current. I threw up my hand and fortunately grasped a spare oar that was fastened along the outside of the boat. This enabled me to pull myself above the surface and breathe. My felt hat had stuck to my head and now almost suffocated me. Pushing it back I looked around. Not a sign of life was to be seen. The river disappeared below in the dark granite. My companions were gone. I was apparently alone in the great chasm.

But in a moment or two Powell and Hillers, who had both been pulled down by the whirlpool that was keeping all together, shot up like rockets beside me, and then I noticed Jones clinging to the ring in the stern. As we told Powell, after this experience was over, he had tried to make a geological investigation of the bed of the river, and this was not advisable. Hillers and I climbed on the bottom of the upturned boat, and by catching hold of the opposite gunwale, and throwing ourselves back, we brought her right-side up. Then we two climbed in, an operation requiring nice calculation, for she rolled so much with the load of water that her tendency was to turn over again on slight provocation.

We bailed with our hats rapidly. There was need for expeditious work, for we could not tell what might be around the corner. Presently enough water was out to steady the boat, and we then helped Powell and Jones to get in. Our oars had fortunately remained in the rowlocks, and grasping them, without waiting to haul in the hundred feet of line trailing in the current, we made for the left wall, where I managed to leap out on a shelf and catch the rope over a projection, before the *Canonita*, unharmed, dashed up to the spot; her only mishap was the loss of a rowlock and two oars.

Starting once more on the swift current, we found rapids sometimes so situated that it was difficult to make a landing for examination. At one of these places, towards evening, a good deal of time was spent working down to the head of an ugly looking spot which could not be fairly seen. An enormous rock lay in the very middle at the head of the descent. There was no landing-place till very near the plunge, and in dropping down when we came to the point where it was planned that I should jump out upon a projecting flat rock, a sudden lurch of the boat due to what Stanton afterwards called fountains, and we termed boils, caused me, instead of landing on the rock, to disappear in the rushing waters.

The current catching the boat, she began to move rapidly stern foremost toward the fall. Powell and Jones jumped out on rocks as they shot past, hoping to catch the line, but they could not reach it, and Jones had all he could do to get ashore. Meanwhile I had come to the surface, and going to the boat by means of the line which I still held, I fairly tumbled on board. Hillers handed me one of my oars which had come loose, and we were ready to take the fall, now close at hand, albeit we were stern first. As we sped down, the tide carried us far up on the huge rock, whose shelving surface sank upstream below the surging torrent, and at the same moment turned our bow towards the left-hand bank. Perceiving this advantage we pulled with all our strength and shot across the very head of the rapid, running in behind a large rock on the brink, where the boat lodged till I was able to leap ashore, or rather to another rock where there was a footing, and make fast the line.

It was a close shave. The *Canonita*, forewarned, was able to let down to this place, from whence we made a portage to the bottom the next morning. When once started again, we found ourselves in a very narrow gorge, where for four or five miles it was impossible to stop on account of the swift current which swept the boats along like chaff before a gale, swinging them from one side to the other, and often turning them round and round in the large whirlpools despite every effort we made to prevent this performance. In fact, we had no control of the craft in this distance, and it was fortunate that there was nothing worse to be here encountered.

The whirlpools were the most perfect specimens I ever saw. Usually they were about 20 feet in diameter, drawing evenly down toward the vortex, the center being probably about eighteen inches to two feet below the rim. The vortex at the top was about six to ten inches in diameter, diminishing in five or six feet to a mere point at the bottom. Our boats were 22 feet long, and as they were turned around in these whirls they about reached across them, while we could look over the side and see the vortex sucking down every small object. The opposite of these was the fountains, or boils, where the surface was exactly the reverse of the whirls: a circular mass of water about

20 feet in diameter would suddenly lift itself a foot or two above the general surface with a boiling, swirling movement. As I remember them they were usually the forerunners of the whirlpools.

The river was still on the rise, scoring at the last camp another three feet. With such a dashing current the time we made where we were not compelled to move cautiously was admirable. On this day 14 miles were traversed, we ran 23 rapids, and, what pleased us most, we saw the granite disappear, and the comfortable-looking red strata were again beside us. The river widened somewhat, and was now about 250 feet. A cascade was passed on the 7th, which we recognized as one Beaman, who had climbed up to it during the winter, from the mouth of the Kanab, had photographed. From here to the Kanab was ten miles, and we sailed along with lightened hearts, knowing that our sadly depleted and half-ruined stock of rations would soon be replenished, and that mail from the world would be delivered by the pack train we expected to find there. Late in the afternoon we arrived at the narrow cleft, and our men, who had waited long, were overjoyed to greet us once more, for, as we were several days overdue, they had been filled with forebodings, and had made up their minds they would never see us again.

A RIVER MYSTERY

Scott Thybony

The still unsolved disappearance of Glen and Bessie Hyde

FALL, 1928, ALONG GRAND Canyon's South Rim. A Michigan tourist rushes up to a party of mounted sightseers on an isolated overlook. As he catches his breath, he tells the guide the group must go get help, fast. He's seen a boat with two people in it caught in a whirlpool on the Colorado River. It looked as though they were in trouble.

The dude wrangler listens impassively as the tourist tells him what he's seen: The people in the wooden scow had been forced to jump to the bank and haul their boat upriver. At the top of the eddy they'd leaped back in and tried to pole their way into the main current. Each time they tried, the eddy pulled them back. They looked trapped.

The guide isn't worried. Those people had hiked to the rim a couple of days before, he tells the tourist, and they know what they are doing. The sightseeing party continues on its way, unaware that that had been the last anyone saw of the couple struggling to break out of the eddy.

A month later army pilots flying 50 feet above the river spot a flat-bottomed scow. The boat had snagged away from shore several miles below Diamond Creek. It looks in good shape, but there is no sign of the missing couple.

1928, Green River, Utah. Glen and Bessie Hyde had put on the water on October 20. They billed their expedition as a honeymoon trip, though they were married six months before.

The Roaring Twenties were in full swing. Prohibition was fueling an underground economy, police had just seized four million dollars' worth of cocaine, and people were going into debt to maintain appearances. And it seemed that the days of real exploration had given way to dramatic stunts like going over waterfalls in barrels.

The year before, a party had run the Colorado—one of only a handful of successful expeditions since John Wesley Powell first ran it over a half-century before. As a publicity gimmick they took along a pet bear.

Glen and Bessie decided to pull a stunt that would land them a book contract and a sure ride on the lecture circuit. The Colorado was considered an extremely dangerous river in 1928. Their plan was to run it in a homemade boat, in record time, through the most notorious rapids in the world—without life jackets. Bessie had never run a river before, but she was the first woman to attempt the Colorado. Glen was an Idaho rancher with limited experience. He had run the Salmon River and had floated the Fraser and Peace rivers in Canada. When reporters asked him why he wanted to go down the Colorado, he told them he wanted to give his bride a thrill.

The flat-bottomed scow was 20 feet long and 5 feet wide. Experienced boatmen said it looked like a coffin. It had long sweep oars rigged at the bow and stern. To travel fast its two passengers carried a mattress for sleeping onboard and a sandbox they soaked with kerosene for cooking. They could save time by not setting up camp each evening.

Their trip went surprisingly well as far as Phantom Ranch. They hit a number of rocks but didn't damage the boat. Their only serious incident happened when Glen washed out in Sockdolager Rapid.

"We carried no life preservers," Bessie told a reporter. "I admit I was scared to death. I can't remember very clearly all that happened. All I know is that I managed somehow to hang onto the sweeps and keep the boat as straight as possible until my husband could grab the sides. Then I helped him aboard." They nicknamed their boat "Rain-in-the-Face" because it shipped so much water from the high waves.

The pair reached Phantom Ranch in record time. They had taken only 26 days to make it to the heart of the Grand Canyon. Bessie became the first woman to run Cataract Canyon and the upper portions of the Grand Canyon.

They hiked up the Bright Angel Trail to the South Rim to see Emery Kolb, a photographer who had twice run the Colorado. They were worried about what still lay ahead and wanted his advice. Kolb was surprised by the speed they had made. He was even more surprised when he learned they were not using life jackets. He insisted they take his, but Glen refused. Kolb also offered to let the Hydes stay with him for the winter. It was mid-November and the cold weather was quickly approaching. Bessie was interested, but Glen wanted to push on.

Returning to the river, the Hydes met Adolph Sutro, a businessman from a well-known San Francisco family. They invited him to float with them the short distance to Hermit Creek where they had ordered supplies packed down to the river. Sutro was surprised at how carelessly they handled the boat and wondered how they had gotten as far as they had. Bessie seemed tired of the trip. At Hermit she'd nervously demanded they leave the river, but Glen forced her into the boat and pushed off.

Glen's father waited at Needles, California, for the couple to arrive as planned. When they were two weeks overdue, he contacted authorities. After the army pilots spotted the boat, Kolb, together with his brother and a park ranger, rebuilt an abandoned prospector's boat at the mouth of Diamond Creek and pushed into the river.

It was a cold, dangerous trip. At mile 237 they found the Hydes' boat, intact, the bowline caught in the rocks away from shore. Although a foot of water lay in the bottom, everything else looked fine; there was no damage, no sign of violence. Food and clothing were stowed away along with a box camera, Glen's rifle, and Bessie's terse trip log. The last entry, dated

November 30, mentioned bad rapids but gave no location. Since they had planned to write a book, it was odd that no detailed journal turned up. And although Bessie was an artist, the searchers did not find a sketchbook. Everything else was in place, yet the pair of adventurers had disappeared.

The search party continued downriver. Since they had only two life jackets, Kolb's brother had strapped a five-gallon can on his back. At one point they came close to becoming victims themselves. Their boat flipped in Separation Rapids, throwing them all into the cold river. The ranger was pinned underneath momentarily and nearly drowned.

On Christmas Day all hope of finding the couple alive was abandoned. Nothing indicating what had happened to the Hydes had surfaced. Kolb called off the river search. Meanwhile Mormon cowboys on the North Rim of the canyon and Hualapai Indians on the south searched for footprints in the new snow without luck. Tracks, thought to be Glen's, were found at the foot of the Bass Trail by another river party.

Emery Kolb believed that Bessie must have been holding the bowline above Mile 232 rapid as Glen went ahead to scout. The current pulled her and the boat into the fast water, he speculated. When Glen saw her float past he dived in to save her, but they both drowned. Whatever happened to Bessie Hyde, she had been the first woman to run the Colorado River through the Grand Canyon, at least as far as Diamond Creek.

In a statement to the press, park superintendent Miner Tillostson warned "thrill seekers" to avoid future navigation of the river.

A year later the fathers of Glen and Bessie spent three weeks searching the north side of the canyon from Separation Rapid 31 miles upriver to the couple's last-known camp. It was a rough trip. They ran out of food but luckily found a prospector's cache and a trail that led them back to the rim. No clue to the missing Hydes turned up.

1971, below Lava Falls on the Colorado. It was a rough, low-water trip. Accidents had plagued the commercial river party. A young girl on the trip broke her arm in a run through Horn Creek Rapids. The next day she was evacuated by helicopter.

At their camp, a boatman began telling stories of earlier river disasters to distract the group from its own troubles. The oldest passenger, a woman called Liz who appeared to be in her late 60s, took a special interest in the story of the lost bride and groom, the guides said later. Liz, a short, feisty lady from somewhere in the East, had called the outfitter and asked to take the longest expedition available—a 20-day rowing trip. The company tried to talk her out of it, but she insisted. Even though it was rough, she enjoyed it and never complained. The boatmen remember her as being unusually knowledgeable about the river for a first-timer.

During the tale of Glen and Bessie's disappearance, Liz began adding details to the story that the boatmen had never heard. Someone asked her where she had heard all of this. She said she had known the couple before they attempted their trip. Then she began telling her version of what happened. In the middle of her story, wrapped in the mood of the river, she said she was Bessie Hyde. The river guides didn't believe her.

The trip was hard, she told them. Glen was a different person on the river. "He was a son of a bitch who beat me all the time," she told them. She wanted to back out of the trip when they reached Phantom Ranch, but Glen forced her to continue, she said. Things didn't improve in the lower canyon. She knew that her last chance to escape was at Diamond Creek, where a rough road reached the river.

When they pulled in above Diamond, she told Glen she was leaving. He refused to let her go. She then stabbed him with a kitchen knife, pushed him in the river, and let the boat drift away. She hiked out and caught a bus heading east and eventually changed her name.

The boatmen asked if she wasn't afraid of getting caught by telling her story. "I've lived my life," she said, "and nobody is going to believe me anyway."

O.C. Dale was one of the boatmen who listened to her story that night. He still believes she was only joking. But another river guide on the trip, George Billingsley, is convinced there is a good chance Liz was actually Bessie Hyde. At the time she told her story, George wasn't very familiar with the history of the Hydes' disappearance. Yet much of what he has learned about the case since fits the story Liz told that night by the campfire.

The circumstantial evidence is intriguing. Liz is Bessie's age and height; she lives near Bessie's hometown. On her "first" Colorado River trip, she was able to relate a convincing story about Bessie Hyde on the spur of the moment.

Years after her river trip, I called Liz at her home. She was able to recount details of the 1971 trip that the boatmen had forgotten, but when asked about the Hydes' disappearance she denied having told the story. "I don't remember that at all," she said matter-of-factly. "I'm not Bessie. I don't even know the name Hyde."

The real story will probably never be known. Mike Harrison, a former park ranger who had met Glen and Bessie when they hiked out of the canyon, was asked if he thought Bessie could still be alive. He didn't think so. "In those days," he said, "the river never gave up its dead. Never."

V

JOURNEYS ABROAD

TRAVELS WITH A KAYAK

Whit Deschner

A slightly daft expedition to the wilds of Pakistan

YEARS AGO, FROM A WHITEWATER catalog, I ordered an item so insignificant it isn't even logged in my memory. This mail-order company, with an audacious leap of imagination, assumed that I was a rafter and sequentially sold my name and address to several rafting mail-order outfits, which, although I bought nothing from them, still pawned off my name to every outdoor catalog on earth. These dweebs subsequently diversified my supposed interests: I became a gun-infatuated survivalist; I longed for CDs of every imaginable genre of music; I collected cast hand-painted Civil War soldiers. Then my sex was changed so I could crave diamonds and wear lingerie (at least I assumed they had changed my sex) and so on until I had to put in an industrial-sized mailbox just to accommodate this trash. But I got tired of digging through this paper avalanche just to find my bills, so I began a campaign. In the return, stamped envelopes into which I was supposed to merrily deposit my checking account, I instead stuffed rat droppings. I added the following advice: "The enclosed feces are from laboratory rats that may have been used in experiments involving a number of highly contagious fatal diseases. When you are through washing your hands, please delete my name from your mailing list."

136

The effect was immediate, and just when it looked like a junk-mail drought was setting in, a deadly new strain struck. It came in the form of a personalized letter—one that concerned a whitewater trip in Pakistan. It didn't even ask if I wished to participate but assumed I was already coming. Talk about a leap of imagination. The letter ended with, "I've got the boats lined up. Bring a paddle and gear. See you in Pindi, Sept. 21." It was signed Green Slime. There was no sending him rat turds, for not only was there no return envelope there was also no return address. He said he was in Nepal and couldn't be reached.

So . . . I was soon sitting in the Karachi airport awaiting both my flight to Pindi and a chow mein I'd ordered. Although my flight would not leave for two hours, it was looking as though it would beat the chow mein. The restaurant's fluorescent lighting was just bright enough to highlight the grease on the floor, but not so bright that the rat ambling next to the wall was nervous. As I watched the rat slip into the kitchen I wondered if they had junk mail in Pakistan. There was a sudden flurry of activity in the kitchen and soon I had my plate of chow mein. Not that I'm saying it was rat chow mein, it's just that I would have digested the meat more easily had I also seen the rat exit the kitchen.

I don't know what it is about me that seems to attract the kind of people who sit next to me on airplanes. That is unless the maxim—"we are what we eat"—is true and if indeed the chow mein I'd just eaten had had a rat in it. I'd much rather have a philosophical discussion with my fellow passenger, say, "Do you think an anti-abortionist would abort an embryo if the embryo would grow into an abortion doctor?" Or, "How much should the Coriolis effect be factored in for spiraling inflation?" But no, on the PIA (Poor In-flight Alcohol) flight to Pindi, the fellow who sat next to me had a look in his eye that contained the shiftiness of a car peddler, the sleaze of an insurance huckster, and the pushiness of a realtor. And that was just in one eye. I won't even describe the fraud I saw brewing in the other. He said, "What do you do for a living?"

"I sell manure spreaders. I won't stand behind them though."

"I see. That is very interesting. Where are you from?"

"London."

"Ah, nice place, London. You must be a very rich man."

These leaps of imagination people kept taking with me! They were beginning to set distance records. "What makes you think so?" I asked.

"You're flying."

"You're on the same plane."

"But I only come from Karachi."

"You should have taken the bus and saved some money then."

"I think you are a very smart person also."

Another world record! He went on to tell me of his own genius, but what a liability it was being so smart in a country so poor. And, as one genius to another, he asked, "What is your name?"

"Peter Knowles, although you can call me Slime."

"Mister Slime, I am very glad to meet you. I think we should go into business together. We will open the first McDonald's in Pakistan. I have seen them in London. The people who own them are very wealthy. But, there is a problem."

"What's that?"

"I need you to supply me with the money."

"What! And you contribute nothing!"

"Oh no, Mister Slime, I would have a much more difficult problem." I thought this might have something to do with pawning off bacon burgers, or keeping the McRats out of the Big Macs, but no, it was insuring that the cattle were slaughtered in the correct ceremonial Muslim manner. "The customers will get extremely upset if they find out the animals have been killed otherwise. They may start a riot." I agreed that that was a hell of a responsibility and I wondered how I'd explain the fallen arches to my banker. I shook my head sadly and said the deal was off.

The McVisionary shrugged and said, "Maybe you will reconsider Mister Slime. Please let me have your address and I will write you."

"Sure," I said and gave him Slime's London address. "I wait to hear from you, in fact; I wait with bated halitosis."

In the shuffle to pick up bags I managed to lose the McVisionary and hooked up with a Pindi local who wanted to share a cab with me, and sell me on the city as well. He said, "We have clean air in Pindi because we have so few cars. Wait until you breathe the air! Clean!"

But dust hung as thick as fog in the air and the taxi's headlights plying through it rendered an eerie sense, as though the city had just been bombed. The man said nothing. I arrived at our prescribed hotel at five o'clock in the morning. Sitting out in front was a Canadian, Diesel Dave Coles, a clearinghouse of jokes that were most likely illegal in Pakistan. While telling them, we watched the sun rise, and when it had muscled its way through the dust we found and woke up Slime and Marcus Bailie, an Irish spy and distant relation to the Bailey Bridge. Slime, awaiting other trip members, stayed in Pindi, while Dave, Marcus, and I caught a PIA (Perhaps I'll Arrive) flight to Gilgit.

The air in Gilgit was just the way my taxi mate had wanted it to be in Pindi: clean, clear, and cancer-inducing—at least for mates. The women in *purdah*—the ultimate sun block—had no worries. Gilgit's setting was the largest rock quarry I'd ever seen; it was a trundler's paradise, a pet rock sanctuary, and Sisyphus's worst nightmare all bundled into one. The cattle reflected this poor range; they were so skinny that their hides, stretching across their soup-bone frames, looked pre-tanned. The goats, though, were surviving adequately—at least those that weren't having their throats slit by the river's edge.

Picking up our boats, Dave, Marcus, and I immediately set off down the Gilgit River. We all agreed it was an easy float—for the first hundred yards. After that we felt like fought-over kids in a messy divorce between a tidal wave and a hurricane. And conditions worsened when we were involuntarily swept out more than five feet from the right bank of the river. We still have no idea what the run of this river is like along the left bank; however, Diesel says he did see it. Occasionally we stopped for Marcus to take a picture of a bridge.

At the confluence of the Hunza and the Gilgit we were met with a sand-and-trash-laden wind so harassing we had to temporarily pull out. The sky was shredded, the river was tumbling boulders, and the clay cliff we stood under loosened pebbles on us. Diesel nodded towards a nearby village and said, "Whaddya say we go over and watch the veils blow off the women's faces?"

The Hunza was thick, gray, and churning, and when at last we put back on, I said to myself, "Next time I come here I'll go practice first in the back of a cement truck." A clever comparison, I thought, until I looked up "Hunza" in my Oxford Urdu dictionary (OUD not to be confused with the IUD). Translated, it means, "The slosh in the back of a cement truck."

The Hunza frightened us so much that we went up and ran more of it the following day. Still, I can't claim to have boated it. I merely avoided catastrophe, working back and forth in the current next to the bank. I'd never seen such big holes.

"You remember Whit Deschner?"

"Yes."

"It's really too bad. He accidentally fell into a hole on the Hunza, and, well, yes, he did eventually wash out but he's never been able to complete a sentence since . . . "

That sort of hole. Certainly not the place to find the longevity that the Hunza Valley is (thanks to blowhard Lowell Thomas) erroneously noted for. In time, the rest of the group arrived in Gilgit, Green Slime leading as usual from the back, claiming that there has never been a retreat he has been unable to lead. I won't mention any names, but the police register listed our group's occupations as the following: astronaut, indoor yacht instructor, necrophilic, prime minister, suicide bomber, and pile driver. I also noticed in the same register that a Dave Manby had been here several months before us. This Dave Manby however was a poll tax evader. Coincidence, but a paltry one, considering all the Manbys in England—

you know, sort of like all the Shakespeares who wrote plays in the late 1500s.

Early the next morning, we grossly overloaded (two words in Urdu that have never before been coupled) the jeeps and headed up the Gilgit River on an incredible, paved, two-lane highway that gave way 50 feet out of town into something our driver claimed was a road (but I don't think the goats using it believed him). The life expectancy of a jeep driver in Pakistan is about 17 minutes. I have no complaints about the vehicle's air conditioning. The stereo system seemed a bit unbalanced, but this could have been because I spent most of my time hiking out the left side to keep us from turning over. The engine, however, ran worse than a badly tuned lawn mower, and, come to think of it, I push my mower less. We stopped to take numerous pictures, with Marcus snapping shots of bridges, and after a short while—16 hours—we arrived at camp. The dust we had been breathing all day had also settled in geologic layers in our hair and on our faces, giving everyone the appearance of instant aging—which is exactly how we felt. Old and grumpy.

Driving up we had paid little attention to the river's difficulty because, 1) during daylight it was too scary to look at, 2) at night we couldn't see it, and, 3) it didn't matter because Dave Manby had given us his detailed written account of the run.

In the morning I awoke to the sounds of yaks and goats outside my tent. There were also people sounds I couldn't understand, followed by ones I could, like: "What the hell are they staring at?"

Answered by: "If a UFO landed on your front lawn wouldn't you bloody well watch it?"

"I suppose."

"And I'd charge 'em a couple hundred quid for landing rights, too."

At which point some broken English began demanding a couple of hundred rupees.

Peering out from my tent I saw some blue eyes and red heads in the crowd (ones that hadn't come with us), evidence that Alexander the Great got to someone's great-great-grandmom when he came through here. Who gave the Kashmiri goats their golden eyes is a matter of debate.

We piled again into the jeeps and drove to the top—12,250 feet of Shandur Pass which harbors the closest polo grounds to the moon; not only a place where a polo player can die of pulmonary edema but where a mountain climber can be killed by an errant polo ball. Having reached this spot for no apparent reason at all, we turned around, drove two hours back to where we'd just come from, and, in the afternoon, as the sun began to abandon us, we put in on the Gilza, which was merely the upper reaches of the Gilgit.

At first the valley was comparatively wide, a place that seemed to get little reprieve from winter. It reminded me of a tundra river snaking harmlessly through scrub willow, the valley's only trees. Beyond were over-grazed grasses, which dwindled and quickly succumbed to rock on the surrounding mountains. The mountains were lackluster grays and browns except for the occasional telltale mineral colors staining their flanks. Tiny islands of green betrayed springs, but they were all too few in a sea of rocks. The springs were meticulously channeled toward the small pockets of tillable soil, which seemed inadequate to account for and support the number of people who materialized from this vast rockscape to stare at us.

With more abruptness than the local government officials, the mountains closed in on the valley and the river started falling. I am still unsure whether the drops were all safely readable from the river as we eddy-hopped through them or if it was the invading cold that made it necessary to reach our take-out quickly before hypothermia took us out.

The following morning, skipping a steep canyon, we joined the indisputable Gilgit. After paddling for several hours, we crossed a lake. We viewed the place where the river issued from the lake with suspicion, for it held all the necessary ingredients for a catastrophe: a narrowing gorge with a vanishing point somewhere below the horizon. A row of poplars flanking the river diminished quickly to tops, then nothing. I hoped that the distant trees were merely stunted but my hope was quickly exterminated by the unwelcome sound of agitated water. Kids sprinted along the banks with determined purpose for they didn't want to miss telling their grandkids what befell the idiots in kayaks who once disappeared here.

To our jeep drivers who were following us downstream, it was all very funny. As we had paddled past them on the lake, they'd indicated that we were on a collision course with disaster. Two hours later we paddled back up the lake to where they were still waiting.

After our jeep-portage, the river continued to be consistently inconsistent. At least now we had the comforting knowledge that from here on down Dave had run the river, and in our possession was his detailed account. However, turning to it for the first time, we discovered that his advice was written on a single sheet of paper, and that it revealed two unexplained numbers, a "2" and a "5." Considerable discussion ensued as to the numbers interpretation of these. Someone said the river must be a class 2 except for the 5s. Someone else claimed that the class 5 would take 2 hours to portage. Another thought that there were 2 class 5s. Or that there were 5 hours of class 2. And I said that if you multiply two times five and divide it by the number of members in the party, add to this all the loose change in everybody's pockets, and multiply this by the amount of beers in Pakistan, you'll arrive at the average IQ of the group. My point of view, however, was discounted as being sarcastic.

At times the river calmed enough for us to take note of the jagged scenery, but these stretches were not a place we could relax since we knew the river was storing up for some doozy of a drop, like the one where Kiwi Mike Savory got churned in an unsympathetic hole, a Popeye-fight-looking encounter.

Several days downstream, we took a side trip on the unrun Ishkoman, which had probably been overlooked by boaters because of the deceptively flat valley it runs through. The upper section had significant gradient but the water was channeled through gravel and the rapids were of little consequence. However, on the lower portion, the gravel turned into boulders and the water turned into classic rapids. Any more boulders, though, and the rapids would have turned us into classic disasters.

IN THE BELLY OF THE EARTH

Andrzej Pietowski

The first descent of Peru's Colca Canyon, the deepest on earth

PERHAPS GEORGE MALLORY characterized the sensation best when, asked why he had set sights on then unconquered Mt. Everest, he replied, "Because it was there." His terse, seemingly whimsical answer is now legendary—perhaps because it symbolizes the quasi-mystical lure that the unknown, the unconquered, has on all of us. Looking back on the events that led me and my companions— then residents of Cracow, Poland—to the Colca Canyon in the Peruvian Andes, I get the impression that a similar mystical spirit was at work. But unlike Mallory, who found himself drawn toward the crest of the world, we were lured to the deepest canyon on the planet, the belly of the earth, from which cliffs rise more than 10,000 feet.

At first all we had to go on was the suggestion of my friend Piotr Chmielinski—who later became the first man to kayak and raft the Amazon from its source to the sea—that we explore a number of rivers in South America. The idea appealed to us immediately. At the time we were completing our studies in Cracow and I think we all sensed that an era in our lives was coming to an end. We would soon have to accept the "adult" responsibilities of work and family; in short, though we felt confident in our abilities—we had had by then extensive river experience on our native Dunajec and also in many other parts of Europe—we also realized that the moment was at hand for an exceptional adventure. It would be now or never, but where to begin?

In Poland, to even mention that we were planning to explore a river in South America was grounds for institutionalization. Along with the customary obstacles one faces while preparing for such an expedition—plotting courses, gathering supplies—one also has to take into account any number of political obstacles. Poland was, after all, behind the Iron Curtain, with all the attendant problems. Similarly, the political upheavals that constantly plague much of Latin America further complicate matters, a fact well illustrated by the many problems we encountered obtaining entrance visas.

Our first contact with the Colca came in 1978 when we came across an article describing the region. It had been written by Professor Jose Arias, a Spaniard who had developed an interest in the river based on the work of a colleague, Professor Gonzalo de Reparaz, who lived in Lima. The canyon itself was first "discovered" in 1929 by two American airmen who had cleared a small airstrip and flown several exploratory missions over the canyon in a single-engine plane. The airstrip was near the place called the Condor's Cross, where we would later begin our journey.

The entire region was largely uncharted, despite the fact that during the Inca Empire, the Colca River Valley was a vital and thriving center, laced with a network of irrigation channels. Even today one can make out remnants of steep stairways cut into the bare walls of rock, the famous Inca Trail that was used to move armies from one corner of the empire to another, as well as to transport fresh fish from the Pacific to remote Andean areas.

Reparaz, we later learned, had had a keen interest in the canyon for several decades. His interest in the Colca was contagious. In 1978 Doctor Arias as well as Professor Max Weibel of Switzerland made their own cursory explorations of the canyon. Still, their party hadn't included any experienced river runners and thus almost the entire canyon remained unexplored.

Once our initial, vague plans of running rivers in South America crystallized, we set our sights first on the rivers of Argentina. No sooner had we done so when, because of a dispute with the Chilean government over a number of small islands in the Beagle Channel, the Argentine government summarily revoked our visas. We then changed our plans, looking toward Peru and its rivers, especially the Colca.

Already booked on a ship out of Gdynia, we found another unexpected obstacle. This was in the winter of 1979-80, the one winter in a hundred when the Baltic froze. We resigned ourselves to waiting until the sea was once again navigable, but then the military junta governing Peru abruptly revoked our visas. For the first time, after two years of exhausting preparations, we talked of giving up the whole affair. Still, we went on, now looking toward Mexico. As luck would have it, the government there granted us visas almost immediately.

We arrived in Peru in February 1981, via Central America, but we still didn't have a clear idea of how to approach the Colca. The river was there, so were we, but we had little else to go on. It was then that we happened to meet Professor Reparaz himself. He asked us to stay in his home in Lima and, once there, allowed us to examine all of his maps and diagrams. He also infected us with his fascination with the Colca. He was enthusiastic and encouraging, yet we sensed his apprehension about the risks we would face.

It was on May 13, 1981, in a small Andean village, Chivay, 3,600 meters above the Pacific Ocean, that we first heard of the attempt on the life of Pope John Paul II. We managed to get our hands on a battery-operated radio and, in the night's cold—our tea freezing up in our canteens—we listened silently to news bulletins coming across in what seemed all the world's languages. Looking back on it, I believe we formed a pact in the silence of the night. In short, any of us who still might have entertained doubts about taking on the canyon dropped them then and there.

To understand what the death of John Paul II meant to us—we inferred from those early communiqués that he had been killed—I suppose you would have to be Polish. Here was the man who had been raised and later served as a priest and a bishop in our hometown, dying at a pivotal moment of our nation's history. And I now realize that perhaps much of our resolve to go ahead, to take on the canyon, was a kind of self-defense. We believed that through physical exertion we might get our minds off the tragedy unfolding half a world away.

At this time, Solidarity, the movement that had arisen in and spread through all of Poland, seemed to be altering the state of things not only in our homeland, but in a good part of Europe as well. Since we had left Poland we had heard stories about its ascendancy from broadcasts and from sailors, and, to tell the truth, we felt like deserters. But that wasn't unusual considering that, given our nation's history, its shocks and misfortunes, a tradition of social responsibility has become quite pronounced. And it was in the spirit of answering for our actions, I'm sure, that we decided to go on with our plans, to do what we knew best; in short, we would run the Colca, conquer the unconquered.

The next morning, still believing that the pope had been killed by an assassin's bullet, we took a brief, exploratory excursion down to the mouth of the canyon. The river seemed shallow, uninviting. But, by then, it seemed nothing could dissuade us from continuing.

Judging from the charts Reparaz had shown us, the first stretch of the journey would be the most difficult. Here, we faced 44 kilometers of uninterrupted river with no hope of turning back. At the end was a small Indian village, the Canco. From there we had another 56 kilometers to go, though this second stretch, unlike the first, was punctuated with gorges and tributaries that made it possible to leave the canyon. In spite of the fact that the first stretch sloped approximately 800 meters—and this no smooth gradient but a rough course of sudden, sharp falls and cascades—we believed we would finish it in five days.

Looking back on it, I'm convinced that no American explorer would have even glanced at the Colca had his party been as ill-equipped as we were. We had two rather flimsy kayaks, a smattering of pine paddles which, through the run, snapped like so many matchsticks. Our headgear consisted of Soviet hockey helmets. No one had brought a waterproof camera, nor had anyone thought of bringing along a radio. Our most valuable possessions, our movie camera and other photographic equipment, we wrapped in sheets of plastic, convincing ourselves that these were waterproof. Our raft, on which we would pile all of our supplies— a weight of about 500 pounds—was a good one. But worst of all, we hadn't brought any warm clothing, reasoning naively that, after all, Peru has a warm climate.

It was no wonder that, when we packed our supplies and returned to the mouth of the canyon, the German backpackers we met there examined us suspiciously. No wonder when they learned we were about to run the river they began snapping photographs of us, as if we were some peculiar natural formation.

Our first day out was idyllic. We made about eight kilometers, photographing and filming at our leisure. We moved haltingly. The canyon walls at our sides rose three to four kilometers straight up above us, the rock striated, eroded heavily. The landscape, barren and unearthly, reflected an ongoing geological process that probably had begun 10,000 years before with the eruption of a volcano near present-day Arequipa— an explosion that threw into the air a million tons of rock, dust, and lava and subsequently covered the riverbed.

Slowly the river, undaunted, began to break up the thick layer of rock, pushing it out into the Pacific. The signature of this process is found in the striation. Avalanches are common every year, during the rainy season. The settled debris often dams the river, leaving a series of natural lakes. It doesn't take long, though, for the river to push past these dams, to carry the debris out into the Pacific, and in doing so, to pound out new openings in the canyon walls, hence creating new channels along the length of the canyon.

Inside, it's beautiful. One canyon wall is brightly lit, the other left in deep darkness. The temperature difference accounts for the strong air currents that wind through the canyon. They kicked up spray in our faces, at times holding our raft still despite the river current.

Piotr and I are out in front in our two kayaks, like scouts. We stay ahead of the raft, feeling the river out, testing approaches, anticipating rough spots. The kayaks are truly indispensable. They even tow our raft when necessary. And I'm sure we both had every intention of staying in them throughout our run. After all, unlike the raft, a kayak gives one a feeling of safety—its maneuverability promises quick escape, its frame a buffer against the river.

On our second day out our raft overturned suddenly in what seemed a relatively easy rapid. It floated upside down towing the raftsmen behind it right through progressively stronger currents. Reaching down from my kayak, I managed to grab hold of a line and, bracing against a boulder, pulled the raft toward the bank—effectively grounding it. It took me a second to realize that the raft had been towing only three raftsmen and that our fourth, Stefan, was missing. I paddled upstream quickly, blindly, until I finally spotted a yellow helmet, then a red vest, and Stefan himself, naked from the waist down—the force of the water had torn his pants and shoes right off. He was hanging precariously from a rock under a cascade, red-faced but intact.

That was the first lesson. Our second came two days later, on our fourth day out, when the kayak I was paddling was wrecked in the rapids. We hadn't brought any resin with us to repair the damage so, sadly, I left its corpse on an outcropping of rock and took my place in the raft. No safety there. No buffer.

The days passed quickly. We grew more and more tired, realizing that our estimate of five days was way off the mark. Many cascades were simply too risky and we ended up portaging our supplies around them. In addition, the river widened at points to about 20 meters and narrowed to as few as three. At times, our raft was caught between boulders and took in water while we frantically tried to work it back into the current. I was afraid to even think of what would happen to us if the raft were punctured or if we lost our other kayak.

The landscape was truly dazzling. Somehow, I find it impossible to describe—no totally suitable metaphors come to mind. Perhaps "mythical" and "primordial" come closest. Later, on a subsequent trip, we would take a number of geologists with us through the Colca and they wouldn't be able to take their eyes off the canyon walls—those living testaments, those striations that impassively wear the history of our planet's formation. Era after era. Age after age. Period after period. Unlike those geologists, I took a more active interest in the many rock towers thrusting out from the river, stretching for kilometers at a time, seemingly frozen in space. A number of these resembled sculptures. I made out a child's head in one, a camel in another and, the most mysterious, a remarkably intricate castle with two rocky towers.

Often we spied steam rising from a hot spring. Geologically, the area is full of activity, despite its barren appearance. One familiar element was the strip of blue we saw above, very high up, but too often it took on a strange character, dotted more and more with the craggy silhouettes of condors.

It was on our fifth day out, after a particularly grueling experience portaging our supplies around a cascade, that the stark reality of our situation dawned on us. By three o'clock the sun dropped behind the peaks to our right, it grew cold, and we decided to bivouac. Our clothing, light as it was, was sopping wet. Hanging our supplies out to dry, we fixed supper from the assortment of powders and dried goods we had brought along—mixing them in a large kettle. Our fuel had long since given out and we had to resort to gathering whatever sticks we could find for a fire. It seemed that nothing grew along the Colca—for five days we hadn't seen a single scrap of vegetation—and we knew that we would have to rely on our own provisions.

But this had been measured out with a druggist's concern for quantity, and it was on that day, wet, tired beyond belief, that we realized that if we didn't pick up our pace we could simply die of hunger.

Our talk, as it often did, turned to food. Someone reminisced about some wonderful pastries he had had at a hotel in Cracow. Talking about food seemed our favorite pastime, besides, perhaps, keeping our eyes fixed on the sheer walls above, whenever we stopped, watching for the first signs of an avalanche. A minor tectonic nudge would have meant the end of us.

During that time, two dreams kept recurring in my sleep. In the first, we are being buried in an avalanche and in the second I'm drifting downriver and unable to stop, and I can hear the roar of a waterfall, growing louder at every instant. My companions reported similar dreams.

As time passed, the condors grew more and more daring. Our only consolation was that if we died these huge birds would hardly have made a meal out of the six of us; we looked like walking skeletons.

After the fifth day, the rest blur together in my mind. The sameness of those days: holding the damaged raft back with all our might while it dances at the top of a falls, carrying our supplies around, making camp, breaking camp, dreaming of avalanches, filming the scenery, noting silently the beauty of the vista revealed past the bend in the river, anticipating danger, the relief of seeing it pass. . . . Skinned knuckles. Sunburn. Our jokes, our conversations. Monotony.

We never spoke of those things closest to us. We never mentioned the most important things. The coldness of the night. Doubt. Faith. The meaning behind experiences. We never spoke; it was still too soon for these matters.

On the tenth day, we spotted a number of hills resembling those we had seen in the photographs taken by Jose Arias—eroded hills marking the location of some waterfalls and then, hopefully, the first settlement.

On the eleventh day, I recall the three cascades over which we carried our supplies on our backs. It was probably the single most fatiguing part of our journey—our Calvary. Suddenly, I spotted vegetation in the distance. Beautiful clusters of green. Is it a hallucination? No, it's real. The end of the canyon. "Land, land," I called to my companions.

We drew closer with what little strength we had left and landed on a small rocky beach. We immediately noticed that behind the foliage bend, eyes were examining us suspiciously.

We understood their fear. These Indians, direct descendants of the Incas, have a marked aversion to water. It is believed that none of the ancient Incas knew how to swim—their mythology included a wealth of river demons. Some of these beliefs apparently persist today. More than once we noted that Andean Indians, leading a herd of llamas home from the other side of the river, would not cross a footbridge after sunset—rather they would make themselves comfortable on the other side, wrap their ponchos tightly around and wait patiently for sunrise. Now, confronted with six strange-looking bearded whites approaching from a side no one in their recollection had ever approached from, they were startled. They had reason to be afraid.

We removed our helmets slowly and called to the Indians in Spanish. This settled their minds. Where are we? In the Canco? Right, right in the Hacienda Canco! We are saved!

They greeted us warmly then, bringing food, as other Indians had centuries before to Christopher Columbus on the shores of America. Whether this was to placate us or if it was because we were so wasted away from hunger, I can't say. There was sweet corn, a white cheese, and, in the settlement where they had led us, eggs. Enough so that we had two each.

Later that evening we got our hands on a newspaper, only a few days old, and discovered only then that the pope had survived. Out of all the joy we felt in that moment we spontaneously named those great waterfalls we had portaged only that morning after John Paul II. Then, we also found a bottle of whiskey in our supplies (whether it was left to celebrate just such an occasion or reserved as a buffer against a worse fate, again I can't say for sure) and drank to our new Indian friends.

After a ten-day rest during which we made repairs, the second 56 kilometers of our journey took us only five days. The terrain was kinder and we were delighted that the turquoise water of the Mamacocha covered boulders in the river, making our journey that much easier and faster. We relaxed, subsequently, and letting down our guard, we were nearly killed in what turned out to be a very beautiful waterfall. Ironically, we named it after Professor Reparaz. Then, everything came to an end. Suddenly, the canyon walls drew back as easily as a theater curtain. The river ran along a flat surface straight to the Pacific. We have a few photographs in which we're making faces at the camera. Was it over? The end? We look worn out, our clothes in shreds.

Before we knew it, we were at the press conference: photographers, microphones. Suddenly our pictures were in the newspapers. We were on TV. People wanted to touch us; they were calling after us. We had an audience with the president of Peru.

Where were we in all of this? What I remember most is one fleeting moment when, floating out of the canyon, we all turned back for a last look, as if we wanted to call back those endless, vertical walls that had towered over us for almost a month. Suddenly, I experienced the feeling of longing, longing for the canyon. It was almost as if we had left something back there—something viable, breathing, some small but living part of ourselves. That longing has remained within me ever since. For this canyon, for another, maybe still unconquered one.

A BOAT IN OUR BAGGAGE

Maria Coffey

A cultural encounter on the Ganges

FOR TWO HOURS WE DRIFTED downstream. Ahead, the patchwork sails of fishing boats billowed in the wind, and on the left bank a host of red flags fluttered from a sandstone bluff.

"I don't want to stop," warned Dag.

Beneath the flags the shore was awash with color, as if a carpet of butterflies had settled on it. As we drew closer we saw a narrow ghat packed with people, who were spilling over into the river. Above them, on the steep bank, rows of pilgrims' huts were hung with lengths of brilliantly colored material, and flower sellers' baskets were heaped with red and orange blooms. The flags were flying from a yellow temple on the top of the bluff, and mud-colored buildings huddled at its base.

"Let's go and have a look," I coaxed.

"I can't stand another village," Dag insisted. "No more questions, no more staring, I've absolutely had it."

"Just for a minute," I persisted. "You stay in the boat, I'll go and buy some chai and samosas."

His resolve softened by the idea of hot tea and fresh food, Dag turned the rudder and we paddled up to the shore, a little way from the ghat. As I hopped out of the boat, a diminutive young man hurried over to me.

154

"What do you want?" he shouted. "How can I help you?"

"I want to buy some food," I told him.

"Come with me! I am Sudraj! This village is Sultanpur! What is your name? Maureeya? Nice name! Come on!"

I followed him up the steps and into a winding, bricked lane. Red dust motes danced in the sunlight shafting between softly contoured buildings. Long-eared goats wandered about, women carrying baskets of steaming dung on their heads sashayed by, pilgrims made their way to the river, singing as they went. Vendors called cheerfully to me from behind their stalls, where the red and orange *sindoor* powder used for *tikkas* had been heaped into perfect little pyramids.

"Here, Maureeyal," cried Sudraj. "Chai! Chai!"

The owner of the chai shop was hunkered on top of his adobe oven, frying *pakora* over the open fire and swatting away flies. He had a bull-like neck, a downturned betel-stained mouth and wild, staring eyes. Brusquely, he thrust a beaker of tea into my hands, then wrapped up several *pakoras* in a banana leaf for me. When I tried to pay him he waved away the money.

"He says it is a gift," said Sudraj.

On the riverbank, Dag was surrounded by men who were incredulous to hear that not only had we come all the way from Hardwar, but that we'd just paddled through the night from Mirzapur.

"Go and have a quick look around the village," I urged him.

He returned elated. "I take everything back," he said.

We asked the men if there was a place in Sultanpur where we could camp for the night.

"Acchha! Acchha!" they cried delightedly, and pointed up to where the red flags fluttered against the solid blue of the sky.

Thinking back to my Catholic days, I tried to imagine how I would have reacted to a pair of scruffy foreigners camped in the church vestibule. It's doubtful that I'd have been quite as magnanimous as the pilgrims who arrived to worship Goddess Sitala and found our kayak and tent parked in a corner of the temple courtyard. They came all day in a steady stream, laden with offerings. They rang a brass bell hanging from the door of the shrine to announce their presence to the goddess, touched blessed sweets to her mouth, lay money at her feet, garlanded her, and sprinkled her with coconut milk. Meanwhile, their children played in the courtyard, wriggling over the dusty stone slabs in a game of "snake" or chasing each other round and round our tent. Things got rather hectic during the noontime *puja*. Clamorous bells were rung and the little courtyard heaved with people pushing and shoving to get close to the shrine. The *pujaris* waved lights and incense around Sitala's small, gold-plated face, and when one of them emerged holding a bowl of burning camphor, there was a mad scramble as everyone reached forward to run their hands through the anointing flame. Another scrum ensued when the second *pujari* began handing out a *prasad* of blessed sweets. In the midst of this frenzy was the temple goat, happily gobbling up dropped sweets and tearing chunks off peoples' marigold garlands when they weren't looking.

The goat was a large bearded male, Billy Goat Gruff in the flesh, but Indianized with sandalwood paste smeared on his forehead. The pilgrims thoroughly spoiled him, reverently feeding him with coconuts, sweets, and flowers. Our arrival left him deeply disgruntled. As soon as the kayak was set down, the prow sticking into what we later discovered was one of his favorite sleeping corners, he began determinedly nibbling on it. And to show his disgust of our tent, he repeatedly head butted it and left liberal amounts of his droppings around the door.

When the noon *puja* was over and things quieted down, I leaned on the wall of the small courtyard and gazed over the Gangetic Plain. After weeks on the river, it was dizzying to suddenly be high above it and have a bird's-eye view of the land we had journeyed across. Water and sand merged into each other, gray on white, to form an empty landscape that teemed with vivid life. I thought about all the paradoxes: the monsoons which swept away homes and laid down fertile soil, the compelling beauty of the poorest villages, the rotting corpses in a river said to have the power of physical and spiritual purification. I remembered the ministry official in New Delhi who had declared us potty for wanting to embark on this journey. I was glad we'd ignored his advice to reconsider our plans. It was a journey that had turned me inside out, challenged every one of my values, and made me question how, or why, I would ever return to the safe world, so bland and pale in comparison to this one, that I'd so long and so smugly inhabited.

My thoughts were abruptly interrupted by Sudraj.

"Maureeya, I see you are now wearing our traditional dress!" he cried, surveying the long loose pants and tunic I'd bought in Allahabad, and changed into inside the tent. "Your husband must wear a *dhoti!* He would look in the mirror and instantly be restored in his self-esteem! The *dhoti* is suiting tall men like your husband. Even I, a dwarf, am feeling so happy when I see myself in a *dhoti.*"

He took us to a small, gloomy shop owned by one of his friends, where he selected a length of fine white cotton and showed Dag how to wrap it around his waist and loop it between his legs.

"Mr. Dag and Maureeya, now you are a fine couple!" he pronounced. "And please tell me: is your marriage love marriage?"

We spent most of the afternoon in Tilak's chai shop. Squatting on his oven, he watched us like a hawk, descending upon us to refill our teacups and our banana leaf plates, crying "Eat! Eat!" and standing over us with a maniacal expression on his face until we passed verdict on the food. When we insisted on paying for all we had, he took the money in a growling fashion.

We were joined in the chai shop by a varied array of fellow customers. Three *saddhus* came in first, and paid homage to the framed pictures of Hindu gods on the roughly plastered wall, hanging garlands around them and flicking them with Ganga water. Settling down on the long wooden bench beneath the pictures, they accepted Tilak's food and drink offerings and then turned to the serious business of smoking ganja. A toothless old village man arrived next, followed by a local dairy farmer with milk for sale in the two buckets suspended from a plank across his shoulders. Finally a suave young man called Pradip came in. He wore Western clothes, said he was from Varanasi, and claimed to be India's breakdancing champion.

"Michael Jackson is my guru," he told me. "He had operation to make him white. Very beautiful now."

Dag was attempting a conversation in Hindi with the old man and the dairy farmer. "*Janver doktar,*" he was saying. "Animal doctor."

The dairy farmer was excitedly waggling his head, while the old man pulled at Dag's *dhoti,* asking "*Kitna? Kitna?*" How much?

"*Ek sau rupees,*" Dag told him. "One hundred rupees."

This information stopped the conversation. Tilak descended from his perch on the oven, the *saddhus* laid down their *chillums,* and everyone gathered around to examine Dag's *dhoti.*

"*Bahut mehenga!*" Too much! cried the old man, and he hurried out of the chai shop.

Tilak remounted his perch looking intensely worried, no doubt anticipating the storm about to break.

"Your husband was cheated," explained Pradip with a bored sigh. "This *dhoti* is farmer standard, worth no more than fifty rupees."

When the old man reappeared with Sudraj in tow, everyone jumped to their feet, and chaos ensued. One of the *saddhus* declared Sudraj to be an honest man, another accused him of being in league with the *dhoti*-seller, the old man shook his staff in Sudraj's face, Sudraj imploringly bleated, "Mr. Dag, Maureeya, I am not a cheating man!" The *saddhus* began arguing with each other, the dairy farmer tried to soothe them, and Tilak squatted on the counter, scratching his belly and giving passersby the "tension" signal, wrapping his second finger over his index finger. After half an hour of this, with no apparent resolution, Sudraj slunk out of the chai shop and everyone else calmed down.

"It has been agree," said Pradip.

"What has been agree?" we asked.

"The problem is over," he insisted, wafting his hand about as if to remove a bad smell. "Now, please be telling me, is it true, as I see on the television, that in America some people are starving themselves to death while others are eating themselves to death?"

"Quite true," I told him.

"And this dairy farmer wishes you to tell him if it is true that in America people are eating cows?"

"I'm afraid so."

He relayed this fact to the dairy farmer, who shook his head in dismay.

SANTA MARIA!

Jamie McEwan

Scouting rapids as an adventure in itself

I AM CRAWLING ALONG A rock ledge on the right bank of the Rio Santa Maria. The left bank, across from us, is a 280-foot cliff, and from the top of that cliff another river is falling on us.

We had heard about this place; we'd been warned by our Mexican contact that if the upper river, the Gallinas, was at a high level, its falling waters would block off the entire canyon. So we had checked the Gallinas before we started our trip on the Santa Maria, three days before. It had been low.

Then last night, without warning, five inches of rain had fallen.

The only thing I can see clearly is the bright yellow of my brother's nylon pants as he crawls along in front of me. A continuous blast of water pellets—it would be misleading to call the stuff spray—hits us from my left. There is so much water in the air that I have to breathe carefully to avoid choking. It's like trying to scout a rapid while someone blasts a fire hose into your face.

The legs before me stop, and Tom shouts something.

"I can't hear you!" I shout back.

He starts to back up, and we retreat to where the ledge is wider. Tom turns to face me, bringing his head over until our helmets touch. Even this close, he has to shout to be heard over the roar of the falls:

"The ledge ends. Maybe you could jump in the water there, swim around the point. But I don't know."

"Let me go out and look," I shout back.

Tom nods. I crawl back out along the ledge, my eyes nearly closed, until I reach forward with my hand into empty space. End of ledge.

There are momentary lulls in the wind, when it is possible to get a glimpse of my surroundings. The trick is to open your eyes at the right instant. From many glimpses I piece together an image of an eddy, a pool of quieter water before me. But with rock on three sides, and the fourth side open to the force of the plummeting Gallinas, it could as easily be a trap as a haven. The rock itself is coated with travertine deposited by the limestone-rich water: no cracks, just a smooth expanse, as if it all had been stuccoed. No footholds.

With just five seconds of calm I could make a reasonable assessment of the situation. But it's hard even to think under that steady drumming. I retreat.

"If you jump in, I'm not sure where you'd climb out again," I shout to Tom. He nods, and we go back to where Andy Bridge and Wick Walker wait by the boats. For the first time since I came to Mexico I am cold.

"We can't portage around this side," I tell them.

"We'll have to go back upstream and climb around the other side," Wick says. "Let's look it over."

We launch our boats on top of the driftwood that is trapped against this shore. The force of the wind is causing waves to run upstream, against the current, and we ride them across the river to the sheltered spot from which we had first viewed the falls.

It was October 1985. From some paddling friends, we had heard about the Santa Maria (located about 100 miles north of Mexico City) and decided to run it. We had arrived at the point where the Gallinas enters the Santa Maria happy and excited from a morning of the best kind of river running. Each rapid, at first glance, had threatened to be unrunnable, but each time we could locate eddies that offered the chance to pause midstream and find the next opening. So we would descend, hopping from pool to pool, darting through narrow slots, dropping over ledges, switching the lead, arriving at the bottom excited by each successful solution.

But the group is sober now.

Looking at the falls from here it's hard to imagine that it could be much of an obstacle. Four main spouts leave the clifftop, spreading as they fall into feathery plumes of spray that look wonderfully soft and cool. The spray boils up against the far canyon wall, rising more than the full height of the waterfall itself. A perfect backdrop for, say, an ad for beer or mentholated cigarettes. It is hard to reconcile the way it looks with the miniature hurricane we had experienced a few minutes before.

Standing on the rocky shoreline, we talk it over, sharing a ration of granola.

Andy wants to try paddling under the falls. "It might hurt, but it won't actually damage you," he concludes, smiling.

Wick says, rather mildly, that he thinks we should climb around. The mildness shows that he's not giving orders, not speaking as team leader—just offering an opinion.

I'm with Andy. "Look," I say, "one guy paddles—the rest go out on the ledge as safety. If the paddler gets pinned against the shore, we can throw him a rope, pull him out."

"All right, let's do it," Andy says, with his never-failing enthusiasm.

"We do have a harness for the swimmer," Wick says. "I don't know, though."

"Are you willing to be the paddler?" Tom asks, looking me in the eye.

"I sure am."

"I am, too," Andy says.

"Climbing around is a sure thing, though," Wick argues. "We could waste a lot of time trying to paddle by, and if it doesn't go, the climb's still going to be a lot of work."

"Well, yeah," I say. "We should sort of agree." I look over at Tom. "What do you think? I mean, only the two of us were there on that ledge."

Tom doesn't reply right away.

I am confident of the outcome. In fact, I feel a little devious, leaving it up to my brother Tom, the bravest person I know, right up to and sometimes over the line that separates brave from foolhardy. He had been up to his usual standards on this trip. Before we started I had secretly vowed to run any rapid that Tom did, but we weren't more than a few hours into the first canyon of the Rio Santa Maria when I'd had to eat that promise.

Later that same day he'd crossed the line into the foolhardy area. I wasn't the least bit embarrassed to be manning a rescue rope while he paddled. The rapid was a double drop, the first onto some shallow rocks, and the second flowing against a vertical rock wall—tough, but runnable. But 30 yards below the second drop the entire river flowed underneath a tremendous, house-sized boulder. It simply disappeared.

There were a lot of strange formations on the Santa Maria. The rock is limestone, easily carved and shaped by the river. We had encountered one large boulder that was hollow, with two small "windows" in the side; we had seen streams that poured directly out of the vertical canyon walls. More than once, we'd seen the river flow under boulders, like this.

These were the kind of spots I didn't even like to look at for too long, because when I look at any piece of water, I start to imagine paddling it. And to watch the water flow into a crack between two rocks and then disappear into a dark hole is to imagine being sucked underground, fighting to get through a passage that would inevitably be choked by driftwood and debris. Not pleasant even to think about.

Nor was it pleasant to watch my brother hit the bow of his kayak hard on a rock at the bottom of the first drop, pop his spray skirt, slam against the wall in the second drop, almost flip, and arrive at the bottom of the rapid with a boat half full of water, struggling to reach the safety of the eddy before being swept into the terminal wall.

There was nothing we could do but shout encouragement. Shout we did. Tom ended up against the rock, only ten feet above the strainer. He poled off hard and paddled to safety.

Later Tom admitted he shouldn't have run that one.

So I left this decision—to run the river under the waterfall, or to climb out of the canyon—up to Tom. If something seemed even feasible to me, then Tommy probably would think it was a piece of cake.

To my surprise Tom votes to portage. "It's so hard to know what's happening in there," he says. "It might just be too strong for us. We have a limited amount of strength, you know. Just so much."

I'm on the verge of appealing to his sense of adventure, his curiosity, but a sudden thought holds me back. Maybe he's right. If Tommy hesitates, there might be good reason to hesitate.

"Well . . . yeah . . . OK," I say. "I don't want to do it unless we agree on it." I look at Andy and shrug. He nods. I feel all geared up for action, and I transfer that energy to the new problem. I shoulder my boat and start for the cliff.

Two hours later I'm at the top. Tommy is 50 feet below me. Wick and Andy and the four boats—three C-1s and Tom's kayak—are all in a cave somewhere below him, and we have ropes strung out all over the cliff. It had been a lot harder climbing than we expected; the cliff was treacherously soft and crumbly, and the trees that seemed to offer inviting handholds turned out to be covered with thorns. Even the tree trunks had thorns.

I put a sling around a handy tree and clip myself into it, then try to figure out which rope goes to Tom, which ones to the boats. All these ropes make me nervous. I'm no climber. None of us are. I'm terrified that I'm going to unclip the wrong one and leave someone unbelayed.

"Send someone up!" I finally yell to Tom. Then I amend that: "Send Wick up!"

Some say that most expert whitewater paddlers are overgrown kids who have never managed to adjust to the adult world. Tom and I, both with children of our own, would still fit that description. But Wick Walker is clearly an exception. It's not just that he has a real career, as a major in the Army Corps of Engineers. It's a whole difference in attitude.

Trips like this, or the one to Bhutan in 1981, don't come off without someone obtaining and studying maps, making local contacts, taking pictures, and coordinating equipment. All of the dull things. It's handy to have an adult around, someone like Wick.

So it's a relief when Wick climbs up beside me. Under his direction we change the belay and start hauling the boats up. Soon the rope starts to wear a groove in the soft limestone, increasing the friction, and the boats hang up on small outcroppings. For a while I just think of it as weight training, a workout. That's while the outer layer of skin on my hands lasts. When I get down to the soft, pink underskin—with a few holes, started by the thorns, all the way through to the raw flesh—it gets harsh. Each boat comes up more and more slowly. The last one gets stuck near the top, and we go through three hard heaves before we get it moving again.

Finally we belay Tom and Andy up. We're nearly at the top of the waterfall.

We carry our boats over one more ledge into an almost tropical forest. I'm the last, walking with my head down, so I'm surprised to see their boats suddenly on the ground before me. I look up. To my right I see empty space, filled with the rising mist. Just on the brink of the waterfall is a circular, shaded pool, perfectly calm, blue, with a large tree growing up from its middle. Before me is the river, the Gallinas, sunlit, tumbling gaily over a series of small falls before taking its final plunge into the Santa Maria.

Grass and small flowers grow on tiny islands in the middle of the river. With the sunlight, the clear water, the shallow, splashing river, it's like paradise. Andy has stripped to his shorts and is swimming across the pool, completing the picture.

I sit down right where I am, pull the boat across my lap, and rummage through it till I find two candy bars: lunch. Heaven can wait.

We spend an hour and a half resting and exploring. Andy comes into his own at times like this: unaffected by the climb, he is everywhere—peering over the waterfall, swimming across the pools, exploring the feasibility of running the various rapids on the Gallinas.

I had arrived at the top feeling grumpy and sorry for myself, but between Andy's enthusiasm and the extra round of energy bars that Wick digs out of his boat (the first two didn't seem to reach my stomach—got diverted to another dimension, or something) I recover enough so that soon I too am wading and swimming. It is a magical spot.

But if we had stayed even another 20 minutes we might have been in real trouble. The descent is wooded all the way, not as steep as the climb, but steep enough that we have to use ropes. We work in pairs, Andy and I on one team, Wick and Tom on the other.

Andy and I reach the bottom first, at twilight. It's a jumbled mass of boulders and carved rock; there is no good place to camp, so we walk downriver to scout the next rapid.

The added volume of water from the Gallinas has changed the nature of the river. The next rapid is not complex or tricky, but it's got plenty of raw power. The current banks off of one shore, slams into a large towering boulder, and rebounds into the canyon's vertical wall. It's getting darker by the minute and Wick and Tom are still descending the cliff.

I hike back up to the bottom of the cliff and shout up to Wick, explaining the situation.

"So, is it all right if we paddle on down and look for a campsite, before it gets completely dark?"

"No. Well—go ahead and paddle the rapid, but wait for us at the bottom."

There is something very spooky about paddling whitewater in the twilight. I follow Andy down the long, sloping approach to the rapid. The sensation of speed is much greater than in the light; dark shapes of rock move swiftly backward against the sky. The hissing of the water against the rock walls sounds very loud.

I pass through a chain of waves as I approach the drop. The water pushes me to the left as I drop over, the boulder is coming up, here is the wave coming off of it; it engulfs me, I lose control and flip. While upside down the bow of my boat hits the boulder, then I roll up—and here is the right shore, passing by.

I'm through. I feel more like a piece of driftwood than an experienced paddler in control, but who cares, I'm through.

Andy and I pull into an eddy below the rapid and talk quietly for a moment. The canyon is dark, its rock walls offering no place to camp, but there is still light and color in the sky.

"Tell you what," I say. "You paddle down and find a campsite, get a fire started. I'll hike back up and talk to Wick and Tom."

I climb and hike back upstream, using my flashlight to pick my way among the boulders. Wick and Tom have just arrived at the bottom of the cliff when I get there.

Wick doesn't seem too pleased about the idea of running the rapid in the dark. It's truly dark now; the stars are out.

"Well, you could portage, but it would be hard with the boats."

"Just shut off the light; let us get our night vision." Tom says.

I walk to the river's edge with them, show them where we put in. I tell them how to run the rapid.

I don't mention that it had knocked me over.

We stay up later than usual around the campfire that night, even though we know we'll have to cover 30 miles the next day. It should be an easy paddle, especially in comparison to what has come before. There is a feeling that the adventure is over.

We talk about the trip, trying to sort out the different days to fix them in our memories. It's hard to recall, hard to separate the miles of whitewater that flowed one into another. Instead, we identify the days by remembering the failures, the times we had to carry four portages on day one, including the long one where Wick had disappeared for a time under a jumble of boulders. Three on day two. None on day three, the day of what we called the "Maze Rapids." And only one, but what a one, today.

"You know," Wick says, "it was a good thing we had that climb thrown in there. Otherwise, it all would have been too routine."

"Yeah, and we wouldn't have seen the top of the falls," Andy adds.

I almost protest. My hands are throbbing, my back is sore, and we still have 30 miles to go. But then, maybe they're right. If being comfortable were our first priority, after all, none of us would be here.

Besides, I have learned a valuable lesson. Something I wouldn't have learned anywhere else. Nothing uplifting, or profound. Nothing earth-shattering. But simple enough to be passed along, to become part of paddling lore:

If you're going to scout a waterfall, bring along a diving mask.

VI

OUT TO SEA

ALONE AT SEA

Hannes Lindermann

Across the Atlantic, alone, in a store-bought Klepper

NOVEMBER 19TH

The night was endless. Heavy dark storm clouds would not let the daylight through: only rain squalls, thunder, lightning, and bailing kept me alert. As I expected and feared, I lost my rudder. The steering cables responded heavily to my feet, then suddenly they turned light to the touch, letting me know the rudder had left me. Fortunately I had brought a spare. I dug my chronometer out from its rubber bag and checked the time. Daylight was half an hour overdue.

It came at last, but the monotony of dark-gray skies between masses of heaving gray-green water remained unbroken. Without a rudder, the *Liberia* could not hold a course to the waves, so I shipped even more water. My hands looked bad. I peeled off the sodden calluses.

The rise and fall of the boat during the night had made it hard for me to rest. I was still very, very tired. I crouched and laid my head on the washboard, too frightened to sleep, and as I lay there I heard the spray cover whisper to me.

"Now come," it said, "be reasonable and lie down. Forget everything. Leave it. Let others do something. You don't have to do everything."

At first this conversation seemed perfectly normal, until I remembered I was alone on board. Often, as I awoke, I looked around for my companion, not realizing at once that there was nobody else with me. My sense of reality had changed in an odd way. I spoke to myself, of course, and I talked to the sails and the outrigger, but the noises around me also belonged to human beings; the breaking sea snorted at me, whistled, called to me, shouted, and breathed at me with the rage and fury of a living being.

I had to wait for the storm to lessen before putting on my spare rudder. The sky still threatened. From time to time it thundered and lightninged; tropical downpours and combers emptied buckets of water into the boat. I bailed mechanically and patiently. I gave up worry and thought. The storm had shown me that I could have confidence in my boat. It is only after a man has lived through a storm with his boat that he knows exactly what to expect from her.

NOVEMBER 20TH

This was my thirty-second day at sea. The night was restless, but the wind had weakened. I decided to replace the rudder. With the wick of the rudder between my teeth and the blade tied to my right wrist, I slipped, fully dressed, into the water. The waves were still 15 to 20 feet high, the temperature of the water lukewarm. With difficulty I swam to the stern. One moment I was under the stern, then the boat hit my head, and the next instant the stern was before me. So I took the stern firmly under my left arm, changed the rudder blade into my left hand, when suddenly a big wave tore it away. I cannot describe the shock; it was unimaginable. I reacted quickly, grabbed for the blade and luckily caught hold of the string attached to it. I could feel the sweat of delayed fright coming up inside me. The next attempt was successful: with my right hand I pushed in the wick, fastened it once more with string, and crawled back into the boat. I tried to undress, but the seas, with winds still blowing at 25 miles an hour, were too high. Water had entered the boat while I worked on the rudder, dragging the cushions out of place. I righted them and sat down again. With the steering cables I again controlled the rudder. My new rudder was the standard size, whereas the one I had lost in the storm was only two-thirds as big. Back in Las Palmas I had decided that my heavily loaded boat did not need a whole blade and that a standard size would exert too much pull on the rubber stern. I pulled in the sea anchor, fastened it behind the mizzenmast, and set the little square sail.

Now my legs shook from delayed shock. It would take time for my nerves to calm down. But I felt as though I had won a battle, and after the bailing was finished, I treated myself to an extra portion of milk. The seas still roared around me, the wind blew furiously across a slightly clearer sky. The sun was circled by a big rainbow, a sign of intense humidity in the atmosphere.

NOVEMBER 23RD

Little by little, the wind eased. I hoisted the gaff sail. But the weather did not improve. Squalls chased each other across the water, squeezing rain out of the clouds onto the suffering foldboat below. Every few minutes I looked behind the mizzen to be sure that no bad squall approached, which would force me to take down the big sail. A chart of my course would have looked like the movements of a snake. I was 30 degrees too far to starboard one minute; in the next, a wave pushed me 30 degrees to the south on the port side: but on the whole I managed to keep west.

Two great big dolphins had followed me for several days. Whenever the wind abated. they beat their tails against the bottom of the boat and then swam slowly off. They could easily be caught, I thought, especially when their heads came above water. Though I knew they were too big for my boat, I had a strong desire to get one. I loaded the underwater gun. My first shot was a bull's-eye. The arrow landed on the fish's skull. He jumped, he leaped into the air and lifted the outrigger as he did so. Quickly I jerked at the line and held an empty arrow in my hand. The hooks of the arrow had not taken hold in the hard skull. Perhaps it was better this way!

As the sun went down, 1,400 miles from the Canary Islands, I saw a butterfly flutter in the air. Only the trade winds could have brought it this far.

My knees had improved!

NOVEMBER 24TH

Tropic birds, Mediterranean shearwaters, petrels, and Manx shearwaters flew around me again. The wind was very tired, and all my sails were hoisted. Suddenly, the port-side backstay broke. I took down the gaff sail and, to my horror, saw a huge, dark box only a half mile away. A ship had come up on me without my hearing anything. I had no idea what they wanted. Had they stopped to pick me up? I waved my hands and signaled that I was all right. Evidently they missed my hand signals; I was too far away. They made a turn around the *Liberia*. Stubbornly, I kept the sail hoisted. As the freighter came port side for a second time, I could even distinguish faces on the bridge, crew and a few passengers following with interest my boat's maneuvers. I took pictures and shot film. A young officer jumped from the bridge to the main deck, megaphone in hand.

"Don't you want to come alongside?" he shouted.

"No, thank you," I answered, without giving myself time to think.

"Do you need food?" came the next question, and again I replied, "No!"

He asked my name, and I asked him for the exact longitude. After giving orders to have the bridge reckon the position, he inquired where I came from.

"From Las Palmas. Thirty-six days at sea and with course to St. Thomas," I informed him.

"Would you like me to announce your arrival at the yacht club there?" he wanted to know.

I told him, yes, and gave him my nationality. He gave me the exact position: 56.28 longitude, 20.16 latitude. The young officer found it hard to believe that I didn't need food, but at my insistence the freighter slowly got under way. The captain shouted a last "good luck" from the bridge; the engines started carefully so as not to endanger my fragile boat. Then the steamer, the *Blitar* from Rotterdam, took up her western course.

The meeting left me dizzy. My quick decision to refuse food was unnatural. Evidently my mental discipline combined with the auto suggestions, "Don't take any assistance," had forced my out-of-hand refusal. I thought about their reactions on the freighter as they stumbled on my funny, small craft—which obviously could not hold enough food for a crossing—in mid-Atlantic. The ready offer of help from the captain made me happy. It showed me that men are never alone, that castaways can always hope, and that there are men all over the world who help others.

My latitude was exact, my longitude was a few degrees too far west. Thus even in a foldboat one can take the latitude accurately, although I knew that in a high swell and with heavy weather, it is not absolutely correct.

Tropical rains came down in torrents that night. I caught five quarts of fresh water, perhaps to compensate a little for my firm "no."

NOVEMBER 25TH

A steamer passed at nine in the morning within three miles but with contrary course. In the high seas and winds of 25 miles an hour, they could not see me.

I wondered when the famous stable and sunny trade winds would start. Only at noon did the weather clear for a short time. Another butterfly lay on the water. Dolphins hunted flying fish, and tropic birds circled above the boat.

For the past two weeks some of my canned milk had been sour, but only a little had really spoiled. I discovered some cans with small holes in them and decided that the metal was too thin. The sour milk turned into an excellent aid to my bowels. On a small boat, a badly-functioning digestive system can become a real nuisance. Somehow or other, I had to solve the problem every five to seven days. When I found that my turned milk helped, I no longer worried about the taste.

NOVEMBER 26TH

I counted my pulse rate at night: that night it was thirty-two, lower than the usual thirty-four. My body adapted itself more easily to the hazardous ordeal than did my mind. I was still convinced of a successful crossing, but sometimes I became restless and dissatisfied, cursing at the unstable weather conditions. On my thirty-eighth day, a typical stormy squall rushed to the west. In the northeast, explosive masses of dark clouds gathered.

NOVEMBER 29TH

Yesterday was calm. I shot triggerfish, happy to save more of my food supply. During the night I hung fresh bait into the water: it soon gave off such a strong bioluminescent glow that I could read by its light. In contrast, the meat lying on my deck stayed dark and lifeless.

In the clear blue morning sky, little trade-wind clouds piled up into huge banks of fine weather clouds. The day was warm and windless. On the flat surface, water striders glided over the plankton "dust." A dark remora, the length of a finger, tried to get free passage under the outrigger. It was shy and nervous, darting to and fro between the boat and the outrigger as though denying its stowaway intentions. A little triggerfish showed interest in something on the deck; it turned on its side repeatedly as it swam alongside, looking up at me with curiosity. But it was as cautious of me as I was eager to catch it, and it never came too close for safety.

I was right in the middle of the Atlantic now.

At dusk a swarm of triggerfish swam over to me. I shot two, while the rest stole my barnacles. It was the first time they had eaten off the *Liberia* at dusk, and I thought it might be a school that felt at home with me and my boat.

ON CELTIC TIDES

Chris Duff

Battling the winds of western Ireland

A HALF MILE IN FRONT OF me a cliff rose out of the sea into a gray, overcast sky. Without sunshine and shadow the wall was flat black, no detail or texture, just 200 feet of vertical rock separating the two worlds. According to the map this was Crow Head, the western tip of mainland County Cork. Three miles behind me was Black Ball Head, where the Martello Tower, Britain's response to the fear of a Napoleonic invasion, stood on top of the cliff breaking the smooth line of sky meeting land. The night before, I had camped in the safety of a narrow lough beneath the tower and sat watching the reflection of brightly colored fishing boats floating on a mirror of green fields and blue skies.

Today the ocean was in a different mood, an oily smoothness that wasn't friendly, but neither was it hostile, at least not in the lee of Crow Head. Two miles beyond the headland I could see the tip of Dursey Island, occasional white breakers washing over the rocks along its base. According to the map, there was a channel at the head of the island, a sheltered, direct passage north that would save me from going around the outside, but I wasn't paddling for that point. I wanted to go on the outside, around the tip where the waves were breaking white. I had spent four days trapped by winds that funneled into Bantry Bay and held me tentbound on its south shore. After sitting, writing, going for walks, and impatiently waiting, the winds had shifted from west to north; the close-packed whitecaps laid down to a deeper swell and finally let me out of the bay.

I crossed to the island and paddled close beneath the fields and rock that blocked the winds. It was beginning to rain, and a shiver ran down between my shoulder blades. The north side of the island was breaking most of the swells, but as I drew closer to Dorsey Head, at the western tip, the waves wrapped around the point and the boat began the familiar rise and fall of the swells. The outside was going to be a push. Another hundred yards and I was losing the protection of the land. The high paddle fluttered in the wind, a wave broke over the bow and rolled halfway to the cockpit. With the wind howling in my ears, the sea grew boisterous and lively, and my senses filled with the sights of cresting waves and glistening rock. I felt as if I was moving with an orchestra, listening to the subtle changes of rhythm and tone, and being drawn with the music toward a grand crescendo.

I pulled out from behind the last rock into the wildness of a stormy ocean. The calm of just moments before was blown away with the winds and replaced with a splash of cold spray that hit me in the face and ran into my eyes. I felt the rush of commitment, the exposure fueling me with energy and putting me out beyond the rocks. Six-footers with occasional eight's sinking me into their troughs, then rising above in green blackness. A wave in front of me peaked, the top three feet crumbling with a sound that I had heard too often: a hiss, raspy at first, then growling deeper as it collected momentum and tumbled onto itself, a warning. I leaned into the paddles and moved into deeper water.

Off to my left was a towering thimble-shaped island—bare rock, proud and seeming to dare the winds and sea to throw what they might against its strength. Walls of gray-white, a solidness that looked out of place rising from the sea and thrusting into the air. The island was two miles away but looked much closer, bathed in sunlight by a single shaft breaking through a Kansas tornado sky. A lighthouse, stark white in the sun, so small, against the mass of rock it sat upon, tiny dots of circling birds that must be gannets. The island was Bull Rock, and the smaller island a mile closer must be the Calf. Their names fit the image perfectly, one massive and formidable while the other sat within its protective lee, as if it had broken away but was hesitant to venture far from the larger island's protection. Drifting sheets of rain moved with the squalls across the horizon and moments later the islands looked distant and less dramatic in the absent light.

Between the wave crests and out beyond the Bull and Calf I saw a sharp-peaked island on the northern horizon, then quickly lost it again as I dropped into a trough. A rebounding wave off Dursey Island hit the stern and swung the boat back toward the rocks. A corrective stroke on the crest of another wave and I was back on course, and searching the horizon. Two crests later I saw it again, plus a smaller island a little to the east. The Skelligs? I didn't think they were that close, but there was no mistaking the silhouette of the larger island for anything else on this stretch of the coast. Even from a distance and through the squalls that obscured any detail, the island seemed to leap out of the ocean, pushing skyward not with the gentleness of rounded islands but with harsh lines that shot straight into the low clouds. The larger of the two barren rocks had to be Skellig Michael. I remembered seeing pictures of sixth-century monastic ruins clinging to its side, massive slate steps rising to a shelf of rock, and a cluster of finely built stone beehive huts. Seeing the islands through the squalls and rolling black waters added to their mystique. In a week I might be close enough to attempt a crossing, but I wondered if the seas would allow it. I couldn't imagine a ten-mile paddle in seas like these. I lost sight of the islands again and concentrated on just staying upright.

After an hour of getting tossed around like a cork, I entered the narrows between Dorsey Island and the mainland. I was drained and it felt good to close my eyes and let the current gently spin me in a circle. Rough water paddling was exhausting. The physical exposure seemed to strip away all the protective emotional layers, and I felt as warm as the rocks on the outer coast. In the thick of big breaking waves, it was a constant measure of controlling the flight or fight instinct: too little adrenaline and I won't be aggressive enough, too much and I'll burn up energy too fast. The inclination is to pour on the power and try to get through the rough stuff fast. It doesn't work. The boat charges ahead, then plows into the oncoming wave or crashes into a trough. The only way is to slip into low gear and grind it out. Slow and steady, not fighting the power of the waves but letting them set the pace and hopefully missing the ones that fold over and break on themselves. Dig in, a brace or back stroke here or there, then dig in again. It can be frustratingly slow and fatiguing.

After a brief rest in the channel, I turned and headed back out. Moments after leaving the calm, I almost went over. An inflamed tendon in my right wrist made gripping the paddle shaft with my thumb impossible and I couldn't control the angle of the blade. I had ignored the pain in the rough waters on the outside of the island. Now, without the distraction of breaking waves and a pitching boat, I was keenly aware of it. A wave tossed the boat over on its side and I sliced the edge of the paddle, rather than the back of it, into the water. A last-second hip flick with my right knee jammed against the inside of the cockpit kept me from going over. Despite the tendinitis and the near capsize, I was encouraged by my reaction time. It was instant and automatic, the way it had to be.

Getting thrown over and hanging for that millisecond on the edge, I was reminded of just how tenuous my grasp on the trip was. I had to be "on" one hundred percent of the time and it was wearing me down. It hadn't been a massive wave that had almost upended me. In fact, it had been a ridiculously small one that I hadn't been paying attention to. I had come down off the adrenaline high of an hour earlier and was focused on a cove a quarter mile in front of me, looking forward to getting out of the boat, into warm clothes, and already thinking about how much food and water I had in the rear compartment. I hadn't been attentive to the moment—the worst mistake I could make. It wouldn't have been a big deal to have gone over, but it was a reminder of how a month of paddling had both honed my reactions and also begun to take its toll.

I paddled into the tiny harbor of Garnish, a naturally protected cove that looked as if it would dry out at low water. A couple of thirty-foot fishing boats were anchored at the mouth, their lines hanging loose between bow and buoy. Next to the government pier was a boat ramp piled high with lobster traps and three dinghies pulled above the highest line of seaweed. I landed and walked up to the bigger of two buildings near the water's edge. In the corner of one window was a post office emblem and a stained piece of cardboard with STORE hand-lettered on it. I needed bread and jam, the basics for lunch, and knocked on the open door. An Irish lass with a tangle of red hair, a baby in her arms and another at her feet, greeted me with a smile.

"Hi," I said. "I saw the sign and was hoping to buy some soda bread, if you have any."

"Oh, that's an old sign," she answered. "My mum has some sweets for the kids but I wouldn't know about any bread. Come inside and I'll ask her."

She disappeared into the house, the little guy at her feet hesitating, struggling to keep his balance and staring up at me with huge blue eyes and a dirty, chubby face. We looked at each other for a few seconds, me the giant in the doorway, he the little Irish cherub. I waved my fingers at him and he bolted.

From the doorway and in through another that led to the kitchen, I followed the bare feet and fat little legs. At the far end of the kitchen was a simple table, chairs pulled out as if everyone had just gotten up, and a picture of Jesus on the wall above. A sea breeze ruffled the curtains over the sink and a lady looking just old enough to be a grandmother was stirring something on the stove. "If it's soda bread you're looking for, I haven't got any. But come in and sit down. I'll make ye a sandwich. There's salmon in the fridge and it'll take only a minute." Then as if everything was decided she said, "Yer from America, are ye?"

"Yes, from Washington, on the West Coast."

"And ye here on holiday, are ye?"

"Well, it's a sort of holiday. I left Dublin a month ago and I'm trying to paddle a kayak around the coast. I should be back in Dublin . . . "

The stirring of the pot stopped. She turned, looked me over head to toe, then straight in my eyes, and said, "Ye mean to be telling me ye rowing a canoe right round Ireland?"

"Well, we call them kayaks, but, yes, that's what I'm hoping to do."

The pretty lady with the flaming copper hair came through another doorway with her husband, the babe still in her arms, the toddler clinging to her leg and staring at my feet. The dad, in his mid-twenties, smiled, nodded, and shyly said hello. I suddenly felt like I was on stage, everyone looking at me with expectation. It felt awkward. These people not believing what they were hearing and me still feeling the rush of the morning paddle and the salt drying stiffly on my face.

It was the little guy in diapers who broke the spell and made me smile. I wondered why it was always children that saw the obvious. He didn't care where I had come from or where it was I was going. He was staring at my sandaled feet, my toes covered in sand.

"And are ye alone?"" His mother's puzzled question brought me back to the world of adults.

"Yes."

"Ye came through the channel and not the outside, I hope," the older lady scolded.

The spoon was poised over whatever was in the pot and no one moved an inch. Oh boy, I knew where this was going, but there was no backing out of the kitchen, especially since there was the offer of a salmon sandwich.

"No, I wanted to see what the outside looked like." Then, as a quick diversionary tactic, I said, "But I did paddle into the narrows and saw the cable car over the channel." As if that would somehow excuse me from being a fool and paddling around an island with an easy inside passage. My diversionary tactic didn't have the effect I had hoped. In fact, it sounded pretty weak under the scrutiny of her gaze.

"Ye come around Dursey Head on a day the likes of this?" She paused a second, then pronounced the verdict, "Ye must be mad!"

There it was again. I knew it was coming and thought how I should be counting the number of times I had heard it. The salmon fisherman pulling nets, the shopowners adding sums of penciled figures, the fellow in the pub pulling a pint of Guinness. They each had the same reaction: a look of disbelief, hands frozen in space, and when they saw I wasn't "having on," the inevitable: "Yer mad. Ye know that, don't ye?"

I had little defense to fall back on. I was hoping the baby might cry or the pot boil over, anything to release me from center stage. But no such luck. The verdict was in and I had the right to a final word.

I nodded and with resignation admitted, "Yes, I've actually heard that before."

The woman shook her head, stirred the contents of the pot once again, then dried her hands on her apron. "Ye must be hungry after such a foolish thing. Pull up a chair and I'll make you a sandwich."

In her eyes maybe I was mad, but if it's one thing the Irish are famous for, it's their hospitality—even to madmen. Despite my obvious instability everyone I met wanted to help in whatever way they could. This time it was salmon, mayonnaise, and lettuce. A sandwich and strong tea heavily sweetened never tasted so good. We sat and talked. Mostly about fishing lobster, mackerel, and of course the weather. I heard again how the summer before had been the finest in 20 years. Seven weeks and not a day of rain. The seas smooth as glass and everyone had color in their faces. The little beach had been filled with locals and tourists alike. A Dutch couple, or maybe they were German, were cycling through Ireland and camped on the knoll above the pier. Good thick grass—could stay there if I wanted to. The older lady's brother owned the lot.

"He wouldn't mind if I camped there?" I asked.

"And why would he mind? He lives in Allihies and only comes over to fish. Ye might hear the boats goin' out in the mornin' but no one'll bother ye. If anyone asks, tell 'em ye talked with me."

Two or three cups of tea, maybe an hour of sitting and chatting. An old dog wandered in through the open door, took a look at the stranger, and stiffly walked out again. Life was slow and easy when the road ended at the lobster pots sitting idle on the pier.

I was beginning to like the lazy pace. The sea could wait for tomorrow. I needed a day to rest my arm and the offer of the grassy knoll sounded like a good place to hang out. I camped that evening above the quiet of the moored boats. The smell of the sea, a pile of nets outside the tent opening, and the grass beneath my head assured me that all was right in this little corner of the world.

The next morning, I set out with the wind raising whitecaps on the open water. Looking back at the protected cove, I could see someone standing on the knoll, hands held to their eyes. I remembered seeing an old pair of binoculars sitting on the windowsill near the kitchen sink. I held the paddle on end and waved an arc of farewell, then let the seas surf me over to Allihies—a wild ride across three miles of dancing waters. To the north was Cod's Head, then five miles of open water that was too rough for a safe crossing. The mouth of the Kenmare River would have to wait for calmer winds. I decided to land and walk into the village of Allihies.

I left the boat upside down on the beach and headed up the one-lane road. Out of the wind the sun was warm and there wasn't anyone in sight. A perfect day for a walk. Halfway to town, I passed a gray burro sleepily walking in the opposite direction. He stopped, let me scratch him between the ears, then continued on his way.

A whitewashed cottage with a sign on the stone wall offered tea and scones and a place to sit in the sun. I stepped through the low door and asked for a pot of tea and two scones, lots of butter, then returned to the courtyard to chat with an old man leaning against the warm rock of the house. He must have been at least 80, tall even in his old age, big hands slightly trembling and folded half on his lap. He wore a dark suit jacket, buttoned and covering shoulders that were still wide but stooped. A white shirt and tie, and eyes that closed in warm, safe sleep in the middle of a sentence. He would awaken and ask if I was staying in town. I would explain again that, no, I was just traveling through. Just in town for the day. And again he would doze off.

I wondered who he was. How he had spent his life and what I would be like when I reached his age. Was I his past and was he my future? In that courtyard the same sun warmed us both and so little time separated our ages. I wanted to know him. I drank my tea while he slept.

When he awakened again, I gently asked, "Have you lived here all of your life?"

There was a pause and he answered, "No, no."

I could see his eyes trying to reach back through either sleep or confusion of time, maybe both.

"Where did you live?"

He turned his head slowly to the west and pointed a shaking hand in the general direction of where I had paddled from that morning. Toward the hills that climbed above the bay and looked down on the single-lane coast road.

"Three miles from here. A little farm." His hand came down, found its folded position on his lap, and his eyes closed again.

The day before, I had spent a few hours following the road that cut over the headland and looked down on the island narrows. I thought of the crumbling buildings I had seen. Four walls open to the sky, doorway and windows filling with brambles and making a home for the birds singing in the safety of wild roses and bracken. Maybe one of those houses had been his? Where I had spent a few hours, he had lived most of his life. One old man had lived his life above a small bay looking out on the sea. A young man travels the world looking for adventure and maybe the sense of place that the old one has known. I paid for the tea and scones and left him sleeping in the sun.

KAYAKING THE INSIDE PASSAGE

Byron Ricks

Touching the splendor of the Northwest coastline

MAY   13

At 7:15 a.m. we tune to the VHF weather channel and get no reception. There is also no need. Calm and sun prevail. A deHavilland Beaver, the single-prop workhorse of the coast, glides in over Kootznahoo Inlet, teetering its wings, adjusting, then skimming across the glaze into Mitchell Bay. It is a perfect morning to paddle, but when in Angoon, we must wait for the tide. So, while Maren catnaps, I amble across the rocks to study the torrent. The tide floods, and shoals boil to a foam. A whitewater river has a brighter timbre and is somehow less substantial, even dainty in comparison. A tidal rapid is massive and powerful, with deeper tones in its fury. It thunders. And its surge varies, making it unwieldy and less knowable, a current powered by the gravity of another world.

Gil says there is a trench in the middle of the rapids, and a utility pipe used to run along the bottom. When repairs were needed, when it would be torn apart by the stresses of the tide, divers would have to fix it, able to work for only 15 minutes at a time during slack water. Today our 15 minutes would begin just past noon.

The shore is gouged by current. Inland, the intricacies of Kootznahoo Inlet are low and grassy, with tidal marshes and flats of spruce forest. Among its upper reaches along salmon streams are numerous fishing grounds and summer fishing camps. The tidal rapids guard these places, as they have long done where salmon and herring would simply come to the people—as did we—with the tide. Seaweeds, mussels, and clams were gathered along the intertidal zones, and women and children picked salmonberries, huckleberries, and blueberries by the basketful, dug roots, and scraped the edible cambium and inner bark of Sitka and hemlock, while men hunted bear, beaver, and deer. They often dried food, berry pastes, and fish, to preserve for leaner times. Plants gave them medicines and building material. It was all part of an annual cycle of life, where people lived in permanent winter villages and made seasonal rounds, gathering what they would need throughout the year. Like few other such complex cultures of the world, the Tlingit required little developed agriculture to sustain them. They lived in a luxury of abundance known to few of the more nomadic inland peoples. And until this century, the Tlingit and other native peoples of the northwest coast largely relied, with the exception of small gardens, on what they had learned to gather from the shore and sea.

As we leave Angoon, we paddle past the front of town and drift. From somewhere near this spot on October 22, 1882, the U.S. revenue steamer *Corwin* and the *Favorite*, most likely the same ship that Beardslee had piloted into Glacier Bay in 1880, leveled their guns, then opened fire. It was neither the beginning nor the end of violence, merely an explosive middle that had erupted earlier with similar incidents in Kake and Wrangell. Although many versions of the story are heard, all distill to a misunderstanding among cultures at a time when the American presence in Alaska was young and the territory largely ungoverned.

A general rendition of the story goes like this: A harpoon gun aboard a Northwest Trading Company whale boat accidentally exploded, killing a Tlingit shaman. When the company refused the customary Tlingit compensation of two hundred blankets for the death, the Tlingit seized a company boat, nets, and two crewmen. Still payment was refused. Armed vessels from Sitka arrived, and the people of Angoon were told to pay twice as many blankets themselves for seizing prisoners or the village would be destroyed. The next day it was. We are caught in the gravity of the scene—the small village, rickety from the water, as if still propping itself since that day. Starvation followed in that winter of 1882. In 1973, the U.S. government paid the people of Angoon $90,000 in reparations.

After fighting a terrific headwind, we camp in a cove that holds a deer spine, bear paw prints, and old spruces that were chopped long ago for planks. George Vancouver's crew landed at this same cove for breakfast one July morning in 1794 and met Tlingit looking to barter furs for guns and clothing. Earlier today we passed Killisnoo Island, once a refugee camp for Aleut families displaced during World War II when the Japanese invaded and occupied the Aleutian Islands. Nearly every bay or island or point of land in this often-advertised pristine Alaska wilderness holds a human history, a legacy of many cultures, and their relationships and interactions and traditions are as complex as an ancient rain forest, as the network of inlets, coves, fiords, reaches, and straits of the Inside Passage itself.

MAY 15

The morning is breezy, and we stay in a channel between rocks and a mattress of kelp. It is our narrow paddleway, the kelp softening the waves into a billowing sheen. Kelp leaves stream like ribbons with the current, and they become our windsocks of the sea.

For two days Admiralty Island's shore rises in forested knobs and drops into blue bays shored by moons of white pebbles. We stop often and luxuriate in the midday warmth. It is drier here. Admiralty is in the rain shadow of Baranof Island and receives some three feet less precipitation per year than the sopping outer shores. The idea of a rain shadow is powerful—even one island can alter weather.

We are beginning to read the shoreline well, by chart and by sight, more easily locating landing sites, places that must surely have been visited often in the old days. The canoeing Tlingit valued what we do: steep, protected beaches. Slowly we begin to learn where paddlers have lived and landed before us.

Villages have been abandoned all along this shore, and like many place names on our charts, they carry the parenthetical ABAND. It is a testament to the uprooting that has happened in the last two centuries—native villages decimated by disease, reduced in size then consolidated, then the countless canneries and whaling stations, mining operations, logging camps, various boom-and-bust enterprises. Even today, more people come to travel along this coast than to live.

While expecting to see many brown bears along Kootznoowoo, we have seen only one—a haggard mass—pawing through the tidal boulders last evening. By the time we near Point Gardner, we are thankful to have had quiet nights.

This southern reach of Chatham Strait rolls with silver swells, just perceptible as they lift the kayaks. Exposure grows as we confront the Pacific, its power seeping in between islands. Shores are rugged rock, chewed basalts, with no place to land. Another crossing, our largest, looms ahead—the 12 miles of Frederick Sound.

For several hours, Point Gardner, the toe of Admiralty Island, stretches out before us, lumpy and low, a dragon's snout drowned in the waves. It is a smooth and familiar form. But the great ice has only given a unified look to these otherwise disparate lands that form the Alexander Archipelago and the rest of the Inside Passage. Despite all their seeming permanence, these terranes have drifted north for some 200 million years, gliding with the Pacific plate as if on a conveyor, gradually colliding and melding with the westwardly advancing plate of North America. They have traveled a great distance, some from as far as the Galapagos, and nearly every island is a jumble of geology—limestones shouldering basalts, young rock fronting old—a mosaic at its heart.

As the plates collided, the Coast Mountains rose, scraping moisture from the winds blowing in from the Pacific. Rain and snow fell against the mountain wall, the highland snows accumulating and compacting over seasons into glacial ice that has periodically descended to overrun the lowlands, then retreat. As the Wisconsinan glacial stage of the Pleistocene reached its maximum between twenty thousand and fourteen thousand years ago, sea levels reached a nadir, their water sealed in the vast ice sheets, and the continental margin lay bare. As the ice melted, it unveiled a landscape of rounded hills and smooth valleys that we have been passing for a month now. Sea levels rose and flooded the troughs quarried by glaciers. More slowly, as in Glacier Bay, the land rebounded from the great weight of ice. Eventually salmon populated the rivers, and the beginnings of a temperate rain forest cloaked the land. And somewhere near this time, people appeared.

Debates rage about how they might have first gotten here. The idea that Ice Age hunters moved across the once-exposed plain of the Bering Land Bridge and came to the coast from the interior has long been a dominant theory. But in the past 20 years, some have argued that a coastal route could have been possible when the sea levels were low, that marine hunter-fisher-gatherers could have traveled from Asia into North America along the exposed shorelines.

Although this idea is gaining a following, many coastal Native peoples have oral histories that tell of coming from the interior, of riding the great Taku, Stikine, Skeena, and Nass Rivers through caverns of blue ice to the sea. Rising sea levels and the thick rain forest have all but erased traces of early coastal human dwellings. If evidence is still to be found, perhaps it lies atop the highest peaks and occasional headlands that were once ice-free refugia. And there, some finds are turning up. Native traditions do tell of a great flood, of living atop mountains throughout the region when the waters rose. But some elders have said that this was in a time before this latest rise in sea levels, a time, perhaps, before time.

As in many inquiries, oral traditions and science do not always converge. They are separate entities, hold distinct values. In a region with such complex bedrock, it is unsurprising that people here speak of many stories, many origins.

The ocean swells have intensified. Small, disfigured trees line the shore, and swells belt the rocks. They lift and carry us dangerously toward shore, so we must paddle another two kayak lengths from land. As we round Point Gardner, we are nervous and vulnerable. The water churns, and swells disassemble into high-breaking chop. There is no place to hide. A time to get to know yourself. Squalls, dark lines, race across silver water. A southeast wind howls in our faces. We can do nothing but drop our heads and paddle.

We haven't spoken much all day, focusing on this, the day's major event. At the point we are at a definite place on the map, where the end of Admiralty falls to the sea. The area is gnawed by storms, broken into three fingers of rock and two bays. The first bay, Surprise Harbor, is deep with a flat shore of spruce. The second, where we will stay, is Murder Cove, smaller and more protected, where a Kake Tlingit avenged his brother's death by killing two settlers, an incident that led to the shelling of Kake. Although slack flood on Frederick Sound was less than an hour ago, the ebb is well underway, and we can barely fight the swift river that the sea has become.

Drift logs, fleshy and limbless, are jammed into cuts on the west side of Murder Cove. The chart says TYEE (ABAND). We pass the caved-in buildings of Tyee cannery. Yet in the distance a building is under construction, and we paddle up to its level beach.

While I sit in the kayak, Maren searches for some time before finding the caretaker, who lets us sleep in a rustic loft above the toolshed. He has spent the winter alone, and we are the first people he has seen this spring. "Soon this will be a guest lodge, for people to take it easy out here," he says, surveying the weather-wrapped buildings he has helped construct. "But there is no taking it easy out here."

He is generous but seems nervous by our presence, unaccustomed to living with another's routine. His hair that was once feathered has grown long, retaining only a vestige of its former style. "I'm headed back in two or three weeks," he says. "Then a buddy of mine will come up here."

He opens his kitchen to us, and after we watch *Naked Gun 33⅓* he breaks brown raw hamburger into chunks and sends them sizzling across a skillet.

MAY 16

Weather day.

Dark storms toss Frederick Sound with whitecaps, and all day, rains hammer the metal roof just overhead. Downpours begin and end within 30 seconds, and in the quiet following the rain, the cistern—Tyee's water supply—burbles with fresh rainwater, a coolness that only moments ago was 500 feet above.

Maren and I walk to the old cannery and whaling station, a tumble of weathered clapboard and rusting pistons. Broken bottles of heavy clear glass are embossed IMITATION FRUIT ACID. I put my head into a piston chamber, long ceased with rust and salt. On shore I find a softball-sized float: I AM HERE X. SEND HELP. THIS IS THE ONLY THING KEEPING ME ALIVE.

Back in the caretaker's cabin we find magazines, several months old, stacked near the kitchen table. Three rifles and a new spotting scope rest against a sill. On the wall is an old cannery sign with the image of a mermaid. He found half of it last summer on the rocks and the other half this winter, blown ashore by a cold southeasterly. When I ask about the long winter, he cracks a smile.

"I'm content," he says.

While we have good radio reception, able to hail the marine operator on Baranof Island, we call family on the VHF. It is a quick and startlingly clear call, and I can't help but marvel at this small black box and the invisible circuitry of talk. As we disconnect, I turn to thoughts of tomorrow's crossing, and the outside world again seems distant, nonessential. But in this handheld device lies the infrastructure for our modern world—the filled wetlands, the cut forests, mined hills, smogged skies. It is all here in my palm and undeniable.

The evening is still. Without the customary wind, a shower washes the forest. Clouds on the horizon mushroom with great winds aloft, sprays of thunderhead atop blue cells of power. Conditions must stabilize if we are to cross. I lie awake for hours listening to the cistern trickle full, then overflow.

PADDLE TO THE ARCTIC

Don Starkell

A harrowing tale of survival in the Great White North

WEDNESDAY, SEPTEMBER 16, 1992 (DAY 42)

Fourth day stormbound on McKinley Island in McKinley Bay—near Louth Bay—camp # 26.

12:33 p.m. (noon) Wind howled and blew all night, rattling windows and shaking shack. Skies still dropping more snow, which scares the hell out of me. Wind is so strong it sweeps most of the fallen snow into the surrounding seas. The red windsock on the airstrip is standing straight out. Will I get two more paddle days in before freeze-up? On the thick, meat-freezer-type door of my tiny, insulated bunker room is a sticker, "Do Not Freeze"—very appropriate.

I have been here September 13 to 16—a bad sign. I continue to worry about my food supply and survival. Haven't many options:

1. Stay here and wait till rescue;

2. Get lucky and have a paddle day which could take me within 30-plus mile range of Tuk., and then walk in overland from there, if necessary, without kayak;

3. Wait here till ocean freezes solid enough for walking (say, around October 10?) and then walk over ice to Tuk. (four days) using plastic stretcher for a sled, with kayak on top. I don't have enough food till October 10 (October 1 was to be my emergency final food day on rations). Four days' more walking would take me to October 14.

I don't want to panic, but I don't have any decent walking boots, just my running shoes and my neoprene kayak boots. If walking over ice, I will have to use the latter, which will be too cold. Don't relish walking miles over tundra and freezing waters in running shoes. I've been roaming around this deserted snow island wearing my running shoes inside large plastic bags. I can tent out or sleep in the bucket-like sled/stretcher. If necessary, and if things get worse, I will have to break into the orange housing unit here, which is blockaded at all of the doorways by those heavy crates, weighing tons. The buildings and doors are metal and locked up tight, but I found one partly broken window on the second floor after climbing an attached wooden section. If I need to, I will break into this window. Inside, they may have a canteen and some food supplies left over from this past drilling season.

Around 11 a.m. today I took my first long, cold walk back through a foot of snow to check my kayak, left high and dry on a gravel airstrip. It was in a neglected and sorry mess, all covered in sand, mud, and sea slush brought in by the higher storm tide and winds. It had to be rescued. I returned again with one of the three available seven-foot stretcher sleds found here and loaded my kayak onto it, and brought it back close by, and then into the hallway of my trailer dwelling. Lucky I didn't lose it last night. Damn my carelessness!

I soaked my running shoes in the foot-deep salty shore slush, something I didn't want to do. Praying for sun and warmth and Tuktoyaktuk. Right now am in a very critical situation.

THURSDAY, SEPTEMBER 17, 1992 (DAY 43)

Fifth day stormbound on McKinley Island in McKinley Bay—camp # 26.
5:30 p.m. My fifth sad day here. Very worried. Winter is closing in on me. I'm beginning to believe that I am going to have to be rescued!

The wind blew hard all night from the north and northwest with lots of snow, which has turned my island and the Tuk. Pen. into a dismal winter scene. The thermometer in my insulated room reads 0 degrees Celsius in the a.m., and goes up to 5 degrees Celsius (about 40 degrees Fahrenheit) when I cook.

Scared of my drinking-water supply and fuel running out. My only waterhole was frozen over completely this a.m. with four inches of ice. It is only a couple of feet deep and will soon be solid ice. Knowing this, I broke through and collected nearly 20 liters or quarts of water and filled 80 eight-ounce Dixie drinking cups, and stored another 12 litres in plastic containers found here. It will probably all freeze, but I won't have to go outside for it. Ice at least melts down to almost the same volume of water. The dry, contaminated snow I had been melting came down probably 20 to 1.

The real problem is that melting ice and snow for drinking and cooking will double my daily alcohol fuel requirements from four ounces to eight ounces daily—and I now have only 16 ounces of alcohol left.

Darn it, I only missed by a few days. Today I found an office record showing that some staff were still here September 8, and possibly later. If I only could have made it here five days earlier.

The last two nights I have been sleeping snugly encased in one of the red plastic sled/stretchers, which has an insulated pad and side walls—just like a cocoon. When I'm in it, my only position is stretched out like an accident victim, flat on my back with my arms at my sides. It does give me a peculiar feeling at times, as if I have been seriously injured or am dead in a coffin. But I'm really cozy in my bed at 0 degrees. The temperature outside is much colder.

I found a gallon of paint thinner here, which burns well but with a heavy black, lethal, stinky smoke. If necessary, I can use it for cooking fuel if my alcohol runs out, which will be soon if I don't get out of here. My concerns are still fuel, food, water, and the cold.

Right now very thankful for the extra food supplies I picked up at Bernard Harbour, Cape Parry, and Nicholson-Point. Those two Yugoslavian cook chefs at Nicholson Point sure are lovable guys now. Don't know how I would have reacted to my present situation without the comforting knowledge that I can possibly hang in until October 1, with some very serious rationing. It would be my 57th day from Coppermine.

I still have a fair amount of food, but am scared to eat as much as I would like to as I have no idea how long I will be out here. Mindful that in 1912 Scott of the Antarctic died in his tent, with his four men, only ten miles from their food and fuel depot. I don't want to be another one of those Arctic or Antarctic statistics. If I ever leave here, my biggest necessity ahead will be some sort of abandoned shack or cabin shelter.

I'm still 64 miles from my goal. Just need two more good paddle days. Can't gamble and leave here without the confidence of paddling at least 30 miles to some deserted cabin. Without the protection I have, I just don't know what would have happened to me in these last few days. It would have been very serious. My tent is in such bad shape from the last storm that I hope I never have to pitch it again. Calm winds and seas, please come tomorrow.

6 p.m. Time for bed—rise at 5 a.m.

FRIDAY, SEPTEMBER 18, 1992 (DAY 44)

Breakout from my four-day stormbound delay in McKinley Bay. 8:30 a.m. to 4 p.m. (7½ hours) 33 miles (4.7 mph)—credit only 23 miles (navigation errors?)—Route: from Artificial Island in McKinley Bay to Louth Bay—Atkinson Point, Drift Point, and then to an offshore sandbar camp located 1½ miles north of Bols Point, close to a giant pingo on shore—latitude 69°47.5' north, longitude 131°55' west—camp # 27.

6:40 p.m. Awake at 4 a.m.—all is black and silent. Finally after five days, no snow falling or winds blowing. Conditions cold but near perfect. Waited nervously in the warm comfort of my sleeping bag and four covering site blankets, encased in my stretcher, waiting for the light. At 5 a.m. went into action. Ready to leave at 6 a.m. Went outside trailer and was dismayed to find a heavy fog had set in—couldn't see anything ahead.

With my kayak ready and waiting, I rolled myself back in blankets on stretcher and, heartbroken, returned to sleep.

Escaped at 8:30 a.m., pulling my kayak from its protected berth in the cold hallway of the tandem trailer office. Strangely, it made me think of a torpedo being launched. The kayak was adorned with the decals I found here—"TUK," "Dangerous When Wet," and "Do Not Freeze."

Slid my kayak two yards down the snow-covered sloping sand to the sea. When I started paddling the fog returned, but I had to keep going and chance it. Headed on a bad compass bearing across four miles of open, calm water, to what I thought would be Atkinson Point, marked by a red day-marker. Had to break through soft ice and slush in the shallower waters. Everything foggy and white—all shores and pingos powdered white—almost impossible to distinguish between sea, land, and lifting fog. Lots of shallows.

Fog, bad compass work, ice slush, and then I found a never-ending sandbar blocking my route, extending far to the northeast at Atkinson Point. Backtracked three miles northeast in shallows and sea slush along the damn bar, which seemed to go on forever. Frustrated, I drove my kayak into the bar's mushy shore and then madly waded 100 yards through knee-deep, icy waters. After that I fought my way through a tough, energy-sucking kayak drag over the sand and slush for another 100 yards north to the open sea. At noon my three hours of travel had taken me not that much closer to Tuk. than from where I had started, but I was now out to sea, heading west, and free on the north side of Atkinson Point. I could say goodbye to McKinley Bay. It had been both an island prison and a lifesaving haven.

Killed myself with more tough paddling from noon to 4 p.m. The ten miles of coast from Drift Point to Bois Point were fronted by a sandbank and shallows extending two miles out to sea, forcing me far out from land.

Again I had so much difficulty navigating. Around 2 p.m. I paddled southwest inside and along the south side of a long, narrow sandbar with the mainland two miles away to the southeast. I felt sick, as no exposed ocean sandbar appeared on my map. I was afraid of being again blocked from the sea by this bar, and decided to backtrack to get around its northeast end. But the bar seemed to go on indefinitely so I returned southwest, following my original route, wasting a few more miles. I finally reached the bar's southwest end at 4 p.m.

I was now so tired, and so unsure of my actual location, and in such fear of making another error by paddling to the west and getting trapped somewhere out in the freezing waters, that I believed it would be suicidal to carry on blindly. The temperature was dropping fast, the shores were freezing and "slushing" up, and I was afraid of camping on the nearby mainland shore facing north or northwest, because I could be trapped there by freezing shore slush and not be able to get back to the sea. So against my knowledge and intuition, I decided to camp out at sea on the bar's southwest end. I really didn't have any choice, and I hoped I wouldn't regret it.

Now realize I am in a lethal situation here—on a seven-mile-long, 100-yard-wide low and flat sandbar one and a half miles out to sea running from the northeast to the southwest, facing the northwest, and only two and a half to three feet above sea level, with a two-foot tide in the area. If it storms or blows from the north, waves and tides will surely cover my site. I pray for a calm night. But the skies look stormy.

I picked, with great care, the highest possible elevation for my tent—only three feet high. Placed the rear of my tent to the north, and backed the tent with my faithful kayak as a slight, but helpful, windbreak.

Dressed much too warmly this morning—my light paddling clothes, covered by my borrowed orange drilling-site overalls, and, on top of everything, the yellow oilcloth jacket and pants drilling outfit. Safely in my tent, I removed my two outer layers of borrowed clothing. The orange cotton overalls had kept me warm, but now were soaked in sweat. Vapor rose as I removed them and put them in a corner of the tent. They were soon frozen in an ugly, salty ball, and not again usable. My remaining clothes are also soaked from sweat and paddling. No sun—around the freezing mark and dropping. Not warm enough to dry them. Will have to sleep in my damp clothes and try to dry them out with my body heat. If I take them off they will freeze, too, and I will not get them on again.

Had good supper—only twelve ounces of stove alcohol left (three days?). "Please God—give me a decent day tomorrow." Really scared to be paddling, for the first time in my life, on seas that are starting to freeze. My location after GPS reading—seven or eight miles east of Warren Point. Only 41 miles from Tuk. Just have to get away from here, and fast. With excellent conditions tomorrow, I could make it. Worried!

VII

PRESERVING OUR RIVERS

THE SOUND
OF MOUNTAIN WATER

Wallace Stegner

A plaintive farewell to the wonders of Glen Canyon

GLEN CANYON, ONCE THE most serenely beautiful of all the canyons of the Colorado River, is now Lake Powell, impounded by the Glen Canyon Dam. It is a great recreational resource. The Bureau of Reclamation promotes its beauty in an attempt to counter continuing criticisms of the dam itself, and the National Park Service, which manages the Recreation Area, is installing or planning facilities for all the boating, waterskiing, fishing, camping, swimming, and plain sightseeing that should now ensue.

But I come back to Lake Powell reluctantly and skeptically. For I remember Glen Canyon as it used to be.

Once the river ran through Glen's 200 miles in a twisting, many-branched stone trough 800 to 1,200 feet deep, just deep enough to be impressive without being overwhelming. Awe was never Glen Canyon's province. That is for the Grand Canyon. Glen Canyon was for delight. The river that used to run here cooperated with the scenery by flowing swift and smooth, without a major rapid. Any ordinary boatman could take anyone through it. Boy Scouts made annual pilgrimages on rubber rafts. In 1947 we went through with a party that contained an old lady of seventy and a girl of ten. There was superlative camping anywhere, on sandbars furred with tamarisk and willow, under cliffs that whispered with the sound of flowing water.

Through many of those two hundred idyllic miles the view was shut in by red walls, but down straight reaches or up side canyons there would be glimpses of noble towers and buttes lifting high beyond the canyon rims, and somewhat more than halfway down there was a major confrontation where the Kaiparowits Plateau, seventy-five hundred feet high, thrust its knife-blade cliff above the north rim to face the dome of Navajo Mountain, more than ten thousand feet high, on the south side. Those two uplifts, as strikingly different as if designed to dominate some gigantic world's fair, added magnificence to the intimate colored trough of the river.

Seen from the air, the Glen Canyon country reveals itself as a bare-stone, salmon-pink tableland whose surface is a chaos of domes, knobs, beehives, baldheads, hollows, and potholes, dissected by the deep corkscrew channels of streams. Out of the platform north of the main river rise the gray-green peaks of the Henry Mountains, the last-discovered mountains in the contiguous United States. West of them is the bloody welt of the Waterpocket Fold, whose westward creeks flow into the Escalante, the last-discovered river. Northward rise the cliffs of Utah's high plateaus. South of Glen Canyon, like a great period at the foot of the 50-mile exclamation point of the Kaiparowits, is Navajo Mountain, whose slopes apron off on every side into the stone and sand of the reservation.

When cut by streams, the Navajo sandstone which is the country rock forms monolithic cliffs with rounded rims. In straight stretches the cliffs tend to be sheer, on the curves undercut, especially in the narrow side canyons. I have measured a 600-foot wall that was undercut a good 500 feet—not a cliff at all but a musical shell for the multiplication of echoes. Into these deep scoured amphitheaters on the outside of bends, the promontories on the inside fit like thighbones into a hip socket. Often, straightening bends, creeks have cut through promontories to form bridges, as at Rainbow Bridge National Monument, Gregory Bridge in

Fiftymile Canyon, and dozens of other places. And systematically, when a river cleft has exposed the rock to the lateral thrust of its own weight, fracturing begins to peel great slabs from the cliff faces. The slabs are thinner at top than bottom, and curve together so that great alcoves form in the walls. If they are near the rim, they may break through to let a window-wink of sky down on a canyon traveler, and always they make panels of fresh pink in weathered and stained and darkened red walls.

Floating down the river one passed, every mile or two on right or left, the mouth of some side canyon, narrow, shadowed, releasing a secret stream into the taffy-colored, whirlpooled Colorado. Between the mouth of the Dirty Devil and the dam, which is a few miles above the actual foot of the Glen Canyon, there are at least three dozen such gulches on the north side, including the major canyon of the Escalante, and on the south nearly that many more, including the major canyon of the San Juan. Every such gulch used to be a little wonder, each with its multiplying branches, each as deep at the mouth as its parent canyon. Hundreds of feet deep, sometimes only a few wide, they wove into the rock so sinuously that all sky was shut off. The floors were smooth sand or rounded stone pavement of stone pools linked by stone gutters, and nearly every gulch ran, except in flood season, a thin clear stream. Silt pockets out of reach of flood were gardens of fern and redbud; every talus and rockslide gave footing to cottonwood and willow and single-leafed ash; ponded places were solid with watercress; maidenhair hung from seepage cracks in the cliffs.

Often these canyons, pursued upward, ended in falls, and sometimes the falls came down through a slot or a skylight in the roof of a domed chamber, to trickle down the wall into a plunge pool that made a lyrical dunk bath on a hot day. In such chambers the light was dim, reflected, richly colored. The red rock was stained with the dark manganese exudations called desert varnish, striped black to green to yellow to white along horizontal lines of seepage, patched with the chemical, sunless green of moss. One such grotto was named Music Temple by Major John Wesley

Powell on his first exploration, in 1869; another is the so-called Cathedral in the Desert, at the head of Clear Water Canyon off the Escalante.

That was what Glen Canyon was like before the closing of the dam in 1963. What was flooded here was potentially a superb national park. It had its history, too, sparse but significant. Exploring the gulches, one came upon ancient chiseled footholds leading up the slickrock to mortared dwellings or storage cysts of the Basket Makers and Pueblos who once inhabited these canyons. At the mouth of Padre Creek a line of chiseled steps marked where Fathers Escalante and Dominguez, groping back toward Santa Fe in 1776, got their animals down to the ford that was afterward known as the Crossing of the Fathers. In Music Temple men from Powell's two river expeditions had scratched their names. Here and there on the walls near the river were names and initials of men from Robert Brewster Stanton's party that surveyed a water-level railroad down the canyon in 1889-90, and miners from the abortive goldrush of the 1890s. There were Mormon echoes at Lee's Ferry, below the dam, and at the slot canyon called Hole-in-the-Rock, where a Mormon colonizing party got their wagons down the cliffs on their way to the San Juan in 1880.

Some of this is now under Lake Powell. I am interested to know how much is gone, how much left. Because I don't much like the thought of power boats and water skiers in these canyons, I come in March, before the season has properly begun, and at a time when the lake (stabilized they say because of water shortages far downriver at Lake Mead) is as high as it has ever been, but is still more than two hundred feet below its capacity level of thirty-seven hundred feet. Not everything that may eventually be drowned will be drowned yet, and there will be none of the stained walls and exposed mudflats that make a drawdown reservoir ugly at low water.

Our boat is the Park Service patrol boat, a 34-foot diesel workhorse. It has a voice like a bulldozer's. As we back away from the dock and head out deserted Wahweap Bay, conversing at the tops of our lungs with our noses a foot apart, we acknowledge that we needn't have worried about motor noises among the cliffs. We couldn't have heard a Chris-Craft if it had passed us with its throttle wide open.

One thing is comfortingly clear from the moment we back away from the dock at Wahweap and start out between the low walls of what used to be Wahweap Creek toward the main channel. Though they have diminished it, they haven't utterly ruined it. Though these walls are lower and tamer than they used to be, and though the whole sensation is a little like looking at a picture of Miss America that doesn't show her legs, Lake Powell is beautiful. It isn't Glen Canyon, but it is something in itself. The contact of deep blue water and uncompromising stone is bizarre and somehow exciting. Enough of the canyon feeling is left so that traveling up-lake one watches with a sense of discovery as every bend rotates into view new colors, new forms, new vistas: a great glowing wall with the sun on it, a slot side canyon buried to the eyes in water and inviting exploration, a half-drowned cave on whose roof dance the little flames of reflected ripples.

Moreover, since we float 300 feet or more above the old river, the views out are much wider, and where the lake broadens, as at Padre Creek, they are superb. From the river, Navajo Mountain used to be seen only in brief, distant glimpses. From the lake it is often visible for minutes, an hour, at a time—gray-green, snow-streaked, a high mysterious bubble rising above the red world, incontrovertibly the holy mountain. And the broken country around the Crossing of the Fathers was always wild and strange as a moon landscape, but you had to climb out to see it. Now, from the bay that covers the crossing and spreads into the mouths of tributary creeks, we see Gunsight Butte, Tower Butte, and the other fantastic pinnacles of the Entrada formation surging up a sheer thousand feet above the rounding platform of the Navajo. The horizon reels with surrealist forms, dark red at the base, gray from there to rimrock, the profiles rigid and angular and carved, as different as possible from the Navajo's filigreed, ripple-marked sandstone.

We find the larger side canyons, as well as the deeper reaches of the main canyon, almost as impressive as they used to be, especially after we get far enough up-lake so that the water is shallower and the cliffs less reduced in height. Navajo Canyon is splendid despite the flooding of its green bottom that used to provide pasture for the stolen horses of raiders. Forbidden Canyon that leads to Rainbow Bridge is lessened, but still marvelous: it is like going by boat to Petra. Rainbow Bridge itself is still the place of magic that it used to be when we walked the six miles up from the river, and turned a corner to see the great arch framing the dome of Navajo Mountain. The canyon of the Escalante, with all its tortuous side canyons, is one of the stunning scenic experiences of a lifetime, and far easier to reach by lake than it used to be by foot or horseback. And all up and down these canyons, big or little, is the constantly changing, nobly repetitive spectacle of the cliffs with their contrasts of rounding and sheer, their great blackboard faces and their amphitheaters. Streaked with desert varnish, weathered and lichened and shadowed, patched with clean pink fresh-broken stone, they are as magically colored as shot silk.

And there is God's plenty of it. This lake is already a hundred and fifty miles long, with scores of tributaries. If it ever fills—which its critics guess it will not—it will have eighteen hundred miles of shoreline. Its fishing is good and apparently getting better, not only catfish and perch but rainbow trout and largemouth black bass that are periodically sown broadcast from planes. At present its supply and access points are few and far apart—at Wahweap, Hall's Crossing, and Hite—but when floating facilities are anchored in the narrows below Rainbow Bridge and when boat ramps and supply stations are developed at Warm Creek, Hole-in-the-Rock, and Bullfrog Basin, this will draw people. The prediction of a million visitors in 1965 is probably enthusiastic, but there is no question that as developed facilities extend the range of boats and multiply places of access, this will become one of the great water playgrounds.

And yet, vast and beautiful as it is, open now to anyone with a boat or the money to rent one, available soon (one supposes) to the quickie tour by float-plane and hydrofoil, democratically accessible and with its most secret beauties captured on color transparencies at infallible exposures, it strikes me, even in my exhilaration, with the consciousness of loss. In gaining the lovely and the usable, we have given up the incomparable.

GOODBYE TO A RIVER

John Graves

The joys of canoeing a quiet stream in central Texas

USUALLY FALL IS THE GOOD time to go to the Brazos, and when you can choose, October is the best month—if, for that matter, you choose to go there at all, and most people don't. Snakes and mosquitoes and ticks are torpid then, maybe gone if frosts have come early, nights are cool and days blue and yellow and soft of air, and in the spread abundance of even a Texas autumn the shooting and the fishing overlap and are both likely to be good. Scores of kinds of birds, huntable or pleasant to see, pause there in their migrations before the later, bitter northers push many of them farther south. Men and women are scarce.

Most autumns, the water is low from the long dry summer, and you have to get out from time to time and wade, leading or dragging your boat through trickling shallows from one pool to the long channel-twisted pool below, hanging up occasionally on shuddering bars of quicksand, making six or eight miles a day's lazy work, but if you go to the river at all, you tend not to mind. You are not in a hurry there; you learned long since not to be.

October is the good month. . . .

I don't mean the whole Brazos, but a piece of it that has had meaning for me during a good part of my life in the way that pieces of rivers can have meaning. You can comprehend a piece of river. A whole river that is

209

really a river is much to comprehend unless it is the Mississippi or the Danube or the Yangtze-Kiang and you spend a lifetime in its navigation; and even then what you comprehend, probably, are channels and topography and perhaps the honky-tonks in the river's towns. A whole river is mountain country and hill country and flat country and swamp and delta country, is rock bottom and sand bottom and weed bottom and mud bottom, is blue, green, red, clear, brown, wide, narrow, fast, slow, clean, and filthy water, is all the kinds of trees and grasses and all the breeds of animals and birds that men pertain and have ever pertained to its changing shores, is a thousand differing and not compatible things in between that point where enough of the highland drainlets have trickled together to form it, and that wide, flat, probably desolate place where it discharges itself into the salt of the sea.

It is also an entity, one of the real wholes, but to feel the whole is hard because to know it is harder still. Feelings without knowledge—love, and hatred, too—seem to flow easily in any time, but they never worked well for me. . . .

The Brazos does not come from haunts of coot and hern, or even from mountains. It comes from West Texas, and in part from an equally stark stretch of New Mexico, and it runs for something over 800 miles down to the Gulf. On the high plains it is a gypsum-salty intermittent creek; down toward the coast it is a rolling Southern river, with levees and cotton fields and ancient hardwood bottoms. It slices across Texas history as it does across the map of the state; the Republic's first capitol stood by it, near the coast, and settlement flowed northwestward up its long trough as the water flowed down.

I have shot blue quail out by the salty trickles, and a long time ago hunted alligators at night with a jacklight on the sloughs the river makes in the swamplands near the Gulf, but I do not know those places. I don't have them in me. I like them as I have liked all kinds of country from Oahu to Castilla la Vieja, but they are a part of that whole which isn't, in the way I mean, comprehensible.

A piece, then . . . A hundred and fifty or 200 miles of the river toward its center on the fringe of West Texas, where it loops and coils snakishly from the Possum Kingdom dam down between the rough low mountains of the Palo Pinto country, into sandy peanut and post-oak land, and through the cedar-dark limestone hills above a new lake called Whitney. Not many highways cross that stretch. For scores of years no boom has brought people to its banks; booms elsewhere have sucked them thence. Old respect for the river's occasional violence makes farmers and ranchers build on high ground away from the stream itself, which runs primitive and neglected. When you paddle and pole along it, the things you see are much the same things the Comanches and the Kiowas used to see, riding lean ponies down it a hundred years ago to raid the new settlements in its valley.

Few people nowadays give much of a damn about what the Comanches and the Kiowas saw. Those who don't, have good reason. It is harsh country for the most part, and like most of West Texas accords ill with the Saxon nostalgia for cool, green, dew-wet landscapes. Even to get into it is work. If you pick your time, the hunting and the fishing are all right, but they too are work, and the Brazos is treacherous for the sort of puttering around on water that most people like. It snubs play. Its shoals shear the propeller pins of the big new outboard motors, and quicksands and whirlpools occasionally swallow folks down, so that generally visitors go to the predictable impounded lakes, leaving the river to the hardbitten yeomanry who live along it, and to their kinsmen who gravitate back to it on weekends away from the aircraft factories and automobile assembly plants of Dallas and Fort Worth, and to those others of us for whom, in one way or another, it has meaning which makes it worth the trouble.

Personal meaning, maybe, that includes trips when you were a kid and, with the others like you, could devil the men away from their fishing by trying to swim against orders where the deep swirls boiled, and catfish on the trotlines in the mornings, sliced up then and there for breakfast. . . . And later trips when they let you go out with a friend named Hale and a huge colored man Bill Briggs who could lift entire tree trunks to lay across the fire where you camped under pecans by a creek mouth, above the wide sand flats of the river, and who could fry eggs, rounded and brown on the outside and soft within, in a way you have never seen since . . . Later still, entrusted with your own safety, you went out with homemade canvas canoes that were almost coracles in their shapelessness, and wouldn't hold straight, and ripped on the rocks of the rapids. Squirrel shooting on cold Sunday mornings, and ducks, and skunk-squirted dogs, and deer watering while you watched at dawn, and the slim river bass, and bird song of a hundred kinds, and always the fly-fishing for fat bream and the feel of the water on bare skin and its salty taste, and the changing shore. The river's people, as distinct from one another as any other people anywhere, but all with a West Texas set to their frames and their faces which on occasion you have been able to recognize when you saw it in foreign countries . . . even first bottles of beer, bitter, drunk with two bawdy ranchers' daughters you and Hale ran across once, fishing. . . .

Enough meaning, enough comprehension . . . not the kind that might have ruined it for you, though. It had always the specialness of known good places where you had never actually lived, that you had never taken for granted, so that it was still special when in later years you would come back to it from six or eight years away to find it still running as it had run, changed a little but not much. After the dam was finished at Possum Kingdom near the beginning of the war, it began to filter out the West Texas drainings, and that piece of the Brazos ran clear for more of the year than it had before, and the old head-rises no longer roared down, and the spring floods were gentler and the quicksands less quick. But it was there still, touchable in a way that other things of childhood were not.

The history was in it, too. When we were young we would beg tales from surviving old ones, obscure and petty and always violent tales, hearsay usually and as often as not untrue, and later we confirmed and partly straightened them in our minds by reading in the little county histories and the illiterate memoirs, and they were a part of the river. All the murdered, scalped, raped, tortured people, red and white, all the proud names that belonged with hills and valleys and bends and crossings or maybe just hovered over the whole—Bigfoot Wallace, Oliver Loving, Charles Goodnight, Cynthia Ann Parker and her Indian son Quanah, Pera Nocona, Satank, Satanta, Iron Shirt . . . Few people outside of West Texas ever heard of most of them, and long ago I learned that the history of the upper-middle Brazos was not the pop of a cap gun in the big pageant, but that knowledge never stopped the old names from ringing like a bell in my head.

Meaning, yes.

To note that our present world is a strange one is tepid, and it is becoming a little untrue, for strangeness and change are so familiar to us now that they are getting to be normal. Most of us in one way or another count on them as strongly as other ages counted on the green shoots rising in the spring. We're dedicated to them; we have a hunger to believe that other sorts of beings are eyeing us from the portholes of Unidentified Flying Objects, that automobiles will glitter with yet more chromed facets next year than this, and that we shall shortly be privileged to carry our inadequacies with us to the stars. And furthermore that while all rivers may continue to flow to the sea, those who represent us in such matters will at least slow down the process by transforming them from rivers into bead strings of placid reservoirs behind concrete dams. . . .

Bitterness? No, ma'am . . . In a region like the Southwest, scorched to begin with, alternating between floods and droughts, its absorbent cities quadrupling their censuses every few years, electrical power and flood control and moisture conservation and water skiing are praiseworthy projects. More than that, they are essential. We river-minded ones can't say much against them—nor, probably, should we want to. Nor, mostly, do we. . . .

But if you are built like me, neither the certainty of change, nor the need for any wry philosophy will keep you from feeling a certain enraged awe when a river that you've known always, and that all men of that place have known always back into the red dawn of men, will shortly not exist.

A piece of river, anyhow, my piece . . . They had not yet done more than survey the sites for the new dams, five between those two that had already risen during my life. But the squabbling had begun between their proponents and those otherwise-minded types—bottomland farmers and ranchers whose holdings would be inundated, competitive utility companies shrilling "Socialism!" and big irrigationists downstream—who would make a noise before they lost, but who would lose. When someone official dreams up a dam, it generally goes in. Dams are ipso facto good all by themselves, like mothers and flags. Maybe you save a Dinosaur Monument from time to time, but in between such salvations you lose ten Brazoses. . . .

It was not my fight. That was not even my part of the country anymore; I had been living out of the state for years. I knew, though, that it might be years again before I got back with time enough on my hands to make the trip, and what I wanted to do was to wrap it up, the river, before what I and Hale and Satanta the White Bear and Mr. Charlie Goodnight had known ended up down yonder under all the Chris-Crafts and the tinkle of portable radios.

Or was that, maybe, an excuse for a childishness? What I wanted was to float my piece of the river again. All of it.

THE STRUGGLE FOR A RIVER

Tim Palmer

The death by inundation of a renowned whitewater run

BACK UP AT PARROTTS FERRY,
where we have returned again and again since we first arrived in
Catherine Fox's raft, there is no river in the spring of 1981. The only
sounds are from small waves lapping in the chaparral and in the pines at
a bend in the flooded road, not a bend in the Stanislaus. The campers are
gone. The kayakers and their bright boats are gone. All those barefoot
people in shorts are gone. The field where the June 2 rally was held is
murky deep, and the clump of willows where Gaguine, Grimm, Pickup,
Lynch, and the others chained themselves is a watery tomb. The trees that
Don Edwards, Pete Stark, and Huey Johnson planted in July 1980 are
gone. No boatloads of laughing passengers wash up on that sandy shore,
and no suntanned river guides gather around to drink a can of beer apiece
as they pack up their rafts. The Stanislaus River at Parrotts Ferry is no
longer changing anybody's life. Everybody is gone. Who has come?
Motorboaters, and their exhaust stinks. The place seems full of ghosts,
haunted. But I don't believe in haunted things.

I am looking, thinking about what I don't see, at what is underwater.
At what is dead and gone—for what? California author James Houston
writes, "Economically, ecologically, the history of the far west has continued to be a saga of exploitation, land abuse, bloody struggle, and

215

enormous thefts." Maybe the loss of this river is like the turn-of-century land grabs from Central Valley wheat farmers by the railroads; like the empires of timber amassed by lumber companies under the Homestead Act; like the water rights bought up from Owens Valley farmers; like the diversion of the Trinity River and the death of the Indians' salmon; like Hetch Hetchy.

Above the sick brown shore, I begin walking upriver through the tangled chaparral. I am retreating higher, as people have done for centuries to get away. Go higher and higher to get away from what is happening. Try to get away, then hope that it doesn't catch up with you.

I crawl through oak, manzanita, pines, toyon. Climbing over rocks I watch for rattlesnakes chased from their dens by rising water. I think of Jennifer Jennings, who knew how hopeless this struggle seemed. Looking out to the river, she was stone-still and silent.

"What is it?" I asked, and she said, "Oh, I was just thinking how nice it would be if there was an earthquake." As I scramble, I think of the weight of this reservoir. It is heavy. Ever pick up a five-gallon jug of water? I think of the weight of this reservoir pushing down on the restless California earth. I think of the hanging planters in the Department of Water Resources in the Sacramento office trembling and swaying during the Oroville quake, 70 miles away, after DWR's Oroville Reservoir was filled.

I come to the place where I used to camp. It was a sandy beach with a big ponderosa pine at its upstream end, a flat rock where I'd pile my gear, a shady oak with a fire circle where I'd cook. It is gone and I keep walking. I hear the drone of a motorboat. I pass the house-sized rocks that rose above Chicken Falls, but the falls is deep under, and I see only the summits of rocks where people used to sunbathe and lie and laugh at rafters as they were clutched, then released by the big hydraulic. At Chinese Dogleg, at what used to be the graceful, dancing bend that Catherine Fox loved so well, I cannot see the river, but the surface of the reservoir is agitated. Now and then it quivers and swirls as a remnant of current boils underneath. I am getting closer to the river again, near the upper edge of the rising reservoir. I walk through a flat that is covered with berry bushes, over ground that is lumpy from the work of old miners. I walk closer and closer to the water. The limestone-cobbled shore is dry and untouched by the silent backwater, and up ahead, very faintly, I can hear a sound.

Rapids. The river again. The Stanislaus not yet touched by the dam. The going is rough, and I scramble over, around, and between boulders. Then I see the wild sight of whitewater. Cliffs climb to pointed tops and the Stanislaus curves smoothly around a bar of colored stones. I've made it back to the river.

What I see—this place—has been the main thing for several hundred pages now. The main thing can be babies and children, a warm lover, a friend who reached out and saved you, your soft-eared dog, a job and a paycheck in the bank, your future, the twisted past, war, evil, crops, or God. But here it is this place. Just a river and a canyon and its life. So what that it's the only one of its kind, so what about that irreplaceable stuff. It's just shapes and forms, a low space for water to run, craggy rocks up high, blue sky, sand, stones, sounds, trees, and animals.

Big deal. How can a place do this to people? How can a simple place do what the Stanislaus Canyon has done? I sure don't know. All I know is I feel good sitting here in the sun near the South Fork and listening to the river run by. Why do I feel good? Maybe I was bored and this is different. Maybe I was the opposite of bored, and this is just enough of nothing.

There are powerful places on this earth. Places that uplift people's spirits, as Alexander Gaguine says. He says the Stanislaus Canyon is one of those places. I don't know how this works. There is something here that I cannot hold, but cannot let go of either. Now that this story is almost over, there is something more that needs to be said . . .

Harold Gilliam, a California journalist, writes "To walk by a river or flow with it down rapids and through quiet stretches, to swim in it, to feel on your skin the power of its currents, is to have a direct experience of the flow of time and history and the cycles of the earth that bring the rain and snow, the winds and the waters that flow down the mountains to the valleys and to the ocean again. This is the mystique of the Stanislaus."

Mary Regan, beautiful, crippled Mary, spoke for the disabled who have been to the Stanislaus, "The river and its canyon was our greatest teacher . . . it became for us a wilderness cathedral."

Then there is the other side. When Mark Dubois talked to the Ripon Young Farmers Association and said his spirit belonged to the canyon, they laughed at him.

John Hertle said, "All the talk about a canyon and other things is superfluous. The issue is rafting." Hertle went to China, returned, and said, "They would look at this issue differently. People there don't care about Russia, Taiwan, atomic bombs. The only issue is where their vegetables are coming from. Rafting compared to food to them is utter stupidity."

It was Chief Sealth, from the Pacific Northwest, who in 1854 called the coming of white men, "The end of living and the beginning of survival."

Milton Kramer says this about the canyon: "It provides pleasure. We're so much in pursuit of pleasure that we're losing values that have built the country. It's the sign of a decadent society."

I wonder, is the pursuit of pleasure the same as the pursuit of happiness? You know—life, liberty, and the pursuit of happiness?

This is decadent? I'm looking upriver as the Stanislaus rips around a sunlit bend and picks up the South Fork. A raft drifts into the bend, and the people in the raft paddle and have the gall to laugh while others are working.

I have nothing against a good time, but an important question has been posed: what, if anything, does this canyon provide besides fun?

"It's really hard to find words," Mark Dubois says. "It's not kilowatt hours or recreation days. It cannot be counted, but it is still a value that is important and real to many people. On trips I usually ask people to try to go and sit alone. They return with a glow on their face. They've touched something that they haven't touched anywhere else. This canyon feeds people's spirits."

This is so vague. No matter how you say it, it sounds like thin air. I'd rather just sit on my boulder and not bother, but nobody is going to call me a rafter for wanting to save this canyon. Rafting gets you to some nice places, I'll say that for it, but I'm not a rafter. I'm a canoeist.

Some people believe in nature. That is part of what's going on here. Water cycles, the chain of life, all that. The fact that we're made from earthly elements and when we die, these things go back to the warm ground and feed some other life. It is a belief in life, a reverence for it.

A wild river shows life like no other place. Simple truths of the earth—as Gilliam said—are seen more easily here. That helps to make this place powerful.

Then there is this thing about flowing water. People love it. Maybe some of it stems from being 75 percent water ourselves. Maybe it stems from a heritage of gills and webbed feet. Loren Eiseley said, "If there is magic on this planet, it is contained in water." Whatever magic is.

Alexander Gaguine says, "There is so much beauty and perfection. To realize that it exists adds a huge new dimension to what I thought the world was." Gaguine is coming close. Keep talking, Alexander.

"Trying to keep up with the demand for more water or more power does not uplift people, but spending a day in the Stanislaus River Canyon often does. The experience can raise people's spirits or bring out feelings of wonder and joy. The Stanislaus becomes a very real part of their home, whether people are there for three days or three months.

"I feel that two of the most important things are home and community, and we have both in the Stanislaus River Canyon. It has been the home of people for thousands of years. We can see that heritage more clearly than in any museum, and now the canyon is our home."

On the river, people work as a community and even strangers find themselves helping each other, getting to know each other because of the special demands, the special opportunities that are faced in the canyon.

You don't find that in other places today.

"Europe has its great cathedrals, but in America it is our own great natural landscape which uplifts our spirits and souls as individuals and as a whole nation."

Deep in our past is the ideal of a perfect place. A paradise, an island, Shangri-la. The original garden. It is what many people work toward, whether we think it can be right here or someplace else. To get there is the reason that a lot of people do good. People devote their lives to getting there. Though I have never done that much good, I look at this river and I think I have made it.

The story goes that way back, an apple was eaten. Poor Eve has taken all the blame. What can be so wrong with eating one shiny apple? Even an apple a day. She may have turned around and tenderly planted the seeds, for all we know. It is easy to blame Eve, since she is long gone, but it seems to me we are missing the point. What we are doing now is not eating an apple, but smashing barrels of them into cider that will sour in no time. Eden is being lost today. "What will inspire us when the holy places are gone?" Gaguine asks.

I feel a spirit of the earth. These river people dream that others will feel it too; but here, in this canyon, it is a dream that has not yet come true.

February 1981, Parrots Ferry covered by New Melones.

March 1981, Chicken Falls covered.

April 1981, Chinese Dogleg covered.

Because of low runoff, the level of the reservoir receded through the summer of 1981, uncovering Parrotts Ferry once again. For now, the Stanislaus remains. The other rivers remain, and a very special friend says that you can make a difference.

THERE WAS A RIVER

Bruce Berger

An impassioned reaction to drowning one of America's most beautiful canyons

IT TOOK 20 YEARS—
from the floodgate closing of 1963 to the flood year of 1983—for the lake to fill to capacity and for Glen Canyon to finish dying. Most who flocked to Lake Powell during the first years of its existence were people who regretted, mourned, or were enraged by the loss of the Colorado River. They were also impassioned or cynical enough to take advantage of the access that the rising waters gave them to previously inaccessible caves, ledges, and side canyons. For several years after our trip, Katie Lee explored side canyons in an outboard-powered skiff that seemed to be called SCREWDRIVER until you noticed a small gap between the D and the R, rendering it SCREWD RIVER. While I made numerous camping trips in the Utah canyon country with Katie during that period, I steered clear of Glen Canyon. I didn't want to bear witness to its end, and I put it off with the dread of being roused from a sumptuous dream. For some canyoneers, Lake Powell was simply a truce with reality; for others who discovered Glen Canyon after it had already begun to fill, it was a series of fresh adventures in a new country, new every year as the reservoir rose.

A particularly acute observer of the filling of Lake Powell was Remo Lavagnino, whom I met in Aspen a decade after my trip through the Glen. He had first reached Glen Canyon in 1963, the year the water started to back up. Pulling into Wahweap in the spring of 1963, he rented a rowboat with an 18-HP outboard from Art Greene—and motored to the mouth of the Escalante River without encountering another soul. He and three friends then chipped in on a boat, kept it at Wahweap, and returned to it yearly. The lake was still a mere bloated river and the people were like river people, mostly in kayaks and canoes. His party documented further ecological and archaeological losses as the lake rose.

In a cave up the Escalante River, for instance, Remo found a rock inscribed, in script, "In Search of Nemo." The reference was to Everett Ruess, a 20-year-old poet, artist, and desert explorer who disappeared in 1933 and had been the subject of a nationally publicized unsuccessful search. He had sometimes called himself Nemo, classical Greek for "no man." Inscribed in the slick rock of the same cave was another message about Nemo in French, which Remo couldn't read. Never having heard of Everett Ruess, Remo was startled by the similarity to his own name, as if someone had been searching for him. Knowing the rock would be lost under the water, but fearing it would capsize his low-sided, overloaded boat, he stashed it upside down at the back of the cave with the intention of returning for it later. When he returned with a lighter load, the rock had vanished. Someone, he assumes, still has the rock, while the French inscription lies buried under Lake Powell.

When the lake level had reached some 75 feet, Remo took his boat into the drowned hemisphere of Music Temple and stepped into the cleft that had seemed, in 1962, a nearly imaginary canyon, one that Katie and Natalie had only dreamed of entering. To his astonishment, his party found a ledge barely protected by an overhang, full of artifacts from the pre-ceramic Basketmaker III culture. "We found moccasins, atlatl darts, quids, which were bits of yucca that had been chewed and spit out like tobacco, and a twilled ring basket that was in perfect shape. We didn't know what much of the stuff was when we found it, and half the fun was going to museums later and identifying it by matching it up with known objects. My twilled ring basket is better than the one on display at Mesa Verde. We played in that spot like it was our private sandpile. When we came back the next year, it was ten feet underwater, and everything we hadn't taken was gone."

As the lake rose and spread, Remo and friends noticed a change in the craft they encountered. There was a phase of tiny one-man skiffs, precursors of windsurfers, tacking back and forth in the widening waters. Then came the larger inboard motorboats, models that got bigger with each passing year. During this period, Remo's group was aware of accelerating erosion. Most dramatic was the undermining of sand hills that leaned against cliffs at the angle of repose and collapsed into the lake, creating round, sudsy lagoons and leaving scars where they had shielded the walls. Remo's party, camping well above the waterline in case the lake rose in the night, lay in their sleeping bags and listened to the roar of sand collapsing. By day, they saw rocks turn into islands, trapping animals. Remo found, as if in a fable, an entire island full of mice running around frantically as the water rose. When he returned later in the day, the island was gone. He saw a raccoon marooned on a ledge in a box canyon. When he saw his first rattlesnake in the wild, it was on a sandbar in front of sheer walls, with nowhere to go.

Remo's group would have kept exploring in the low-slung boat, but each year the lake seemed more dangerous. Waves smashed the cliffs and rebounded with no shrinkage in size. There were swells and whitecaps, and the kayaks and canoes had disappeared. As the wind whipped the ballooning water into wilder, more unpredictable tossings, the boats grew until they were yachts and houseboats, with dinghies for plying the side canyons. Watching watercraft broaden was like watching nonbiological evolution. Remo dates the last of his Lake Powell to a particular moment when he saw what looked like an armada bearing down on his party's frail skiff. They stared until they realized it was eight speedboats in a row, each pulling a waterskier who veered back and forth in what seemed an advancing net. "That was the end of our Lake Powell, which was a place for exploration, and its conversion into pure recreation."

By avoiding Lake Powell entirely, I missed Katie's confrontation with the loss of her river. I could only wonder that she subjected herself to that loss. Natalie took one trip with her in SCREWD RIVER, motored over Moqui steps they had taken, powered into Music Temple, and Natalie couldn't face it. "You could take a motorboat right into the place where we had spent the night in the thunderstorm," she complained. "My favorite places were just devastated." They took SCREWD RIVER as far into the side canyons as they could and hiked what was left, leaving the boat mired in a phenomenon known as Dominy Stew, after Floyd Dominy, the feisty chief of the Bureau of Reclamation. The recipe varied, but the daily special might include dead trees, outboard motor oil, styrofoam cups, filter tips, film cans, rotting animals, and the kind of mud we had once tried to claw from our legs. Natalie remembers returning from a hike, coming upon a boatload of fishermen tossing cans overboard, and Katie yelling, "Sit on your ass and catch some bass." Katie doesn't recall the incident but says that she remembers she snapped, "Up yours, dipshit!" to a drunken fisherman at Hall's Crossing with a bitterness the man may not have connected with the loss of Glen Canyon.

After her one trip in SCREWD RIVER, Natalie didn't return until nearly ten years later when the lake was almost full and didn't remind her of Glen Canyon. From 1972 to 1975 she was part owner of a boat at Bullfrog Marina, and she, too, found the lake dangerous. "It was fun but scary. The lake gets the big roller kind of waves. When it's acting up, you'd better just head for shore." It was during that period that all from Aspen who frequented Lake Powell were sobered by the fate of a deliveryman for Railway Express named Ken Ward, who had moved to Lake Powell to run the ferry between Bullfrog Marina and Hall's Crossing. No one ever quite understood what happened, but it was at night and there was a storm. Ken was alone on the ferry. The ferry was found the morning after the storm in battered condition, and Ken was never recovered.

Of the four of us who took the trip through Glen Canyon in 1962, Leo was the least affected emotionally. In fact, he didn't wait for the rising of Lake Powell to seize an opportunity. As soon as we had flown back to Hite, he took off in his Willy's for the set of *The Greatest Story Ever Told* and offered his services as an extra. "They dressed me in this fancy sheet and made me a stand-in for one of them whatchamacallits that trails after Jesus."

"An apostle?" I asked.

"Yeah, an apostle. It was colder'n hell and we spent most of the time in our sheets standing around fires, burning on one side and freezing on the other, then turning around to even it up. Everyone had the flu, and pretty soon that included me."

Leo did return to the area to take more trips with Slim to prospect and look for mementos of Moqui Sam. Then he took up jade hunting in Wyoming and discovered the second largest piece of jade ever found in the United States, 2,200 pounds, for which he found no market because it lacked the cachet of Oriental jade. As to whether he felt the loss of Glen Canyon, his only reaction was, "Boy, all that new water was really sumpn." His friend Slim, however, had considered the river his refuge. As the lake rose he was forced to move into a trailer at Fry Canyon, a tiny settlement near the Happy Jack Mine. But he was not about to let the lake take his two-room house piecemeal, and as the water crept toward its foundation, he dynamited it.

ABOUT THE CONTRIBUTORS

Richard Bangs is author of *Rivergods: Exploring the World's Great Rivers; Whitewater Adventure: Running America's Great Scenic Rivers; Island Gods: Exploring the World's Most Exotic Islands;* and *Riding the Dragon's Back: The Race to Raft the Upper Yangtze.*

Bruce Berger is author of *There Was a River; Almost an Island: Travels in Baja California;* and *The Telling Difference: Conversations With the American Desert.*

Kenneth Brower is author of *The Starship and the Canoe.*

Tim Cahill is author of *A Wolverine Is Eating My Leg; Jaguars Ripped My Flesh; Pass the Butterworms: Remote Journeys Oddly Rendered; Pecked to Death By Ducks;* and *Road Fever: A High-Speed Travelogue.*

Steve Chapple is author of *Kayaking the Full Moon.*

Maria Coffey is author of *A Boat in Our Baggage* and *Three Moons in Vietnam: A Haphazard Journey Along the Coast.*

Frederick S. Dellenbaugh is author of *The Romance of the Colorado River* and *Canyon Voyage.*

Whit Deschner is author of *Travels With a Kayak, Burning the Iceberg,* and *Does the Wet Suit You?: Confessions of a Kayak Bum.*

James Dickey is author of *Deliverance* and *To the White Sea.*

Chris Duff is author of *On Celtic Tides: One Man's Journey Around Ireland By Sea Kayak.*

George Dyson is author of *Baidarka: The Kayak* and *Darwin Among the Machines: The Evolution of Global Intelligence.*

Colin Fletcher is author of *River: One Man's Journey Down the Colorado, Source to Sea; The Complete Walker;* and *The Man Who Walked Through Time.*

Michael Ghiglieri is author of *Canyon* and *The Dark Side of Man: Tracing the Origins of Violence.*

John Graves is author of *Goodbye to a River* and *Hard Scrabble: Observations on a Patch of Land.*

John Hildebrand is author of *Reading the River: A Voyage Down the Yukon* and *Mapping the Farm: The Chronicle of a Family.*

Christian Kallen is author of *Rivergods: Exploring the World's Great Rivers; Islands of Fire, Islands of Spice: Exploring the Wild Places of Indonesia;* and *Riding the Dragon's Back: the Race to Raft the Upper Yangtze.*

Joe Kane is author of *Running the Amazon* and *Savages.*

David Lavender is author of *River Runners of the Grand Canyon.*

Hannes Lindermann is author of *Alone at Sea.*

Bill Mason is a contributor to *First Descents: In Search of Wild Rivers* and author of *Path of the Paddle, Song of the Paddle,* and *Canoescapes.*

Jamie McEwan is a contributor to *First Descents: In Search of Wild Rivers.*

John McPhee is author of *The Survival of the Bark Canoe; Coming into the Country; Crofter and the Laird; Looking for a Ship;* and *Basin and Range.*

Sigurd F. Olson is author of *The Lonely Land; Listening Point; Runes of the North;* and *Reflections from the North Country.*

Tim Palmer is author of *Stanislaus: The Struggle for a River; America by Rivers; Endangered Rivers and the Conservation Movement;* and *Lifelines: The Case for River Conservation.*

R.M. Patterson is author of *Dangerous River; Far Pastures;* and *The Buffalo Head.*

Andrzej Pietowski is a contributor to *First Descents: In Search of Wild Rivers.*

James Raffan is author of *Summer North of Sixty; Wild Waters: Canoeing Canadian Wilderness Rivers; Fire in the Bones: Bill Mason and the Canadian Canoeing Tradition;* and *Bark, Skin and Cedar: Exploring the Canoe in Canadian Experience.*

Byron Ricks is author of *Homelands: Kayaking the Inside Passage.*

Eric Sevareid is author of *Canoeing With the Cree; Not So Wild a Dream;* and *Small Sounds in the Night.*

Don Starkell is author of *Paddle to the Arctic* and *Paddle to the Amazon.*

Gaylord Staveley is author of *Broken Waters Sing: Rediscovering Two Great Rivers of the West.*

Wallace Stegner is author of *The Sound of Mountain Water; Angle of Repose; Big Rock Candy Mountain;* and *Beyond the Hundredth Meridian: John Wesley Powell and the Second Opening of the West.*

Scott Thybony is a contributor to *First Descents: In Search of Wild Rivers* and the author of *Burntwater* and *Official Guide to Hiking the Grand Canyon.*

PERMISSIONS